The
Complete
Limited Liability
Company
Kit

(+ CD-ROM)

The Complete Limited Liability Company Kit

(+ CD-ROM)

Mark Warda
Attorney at Law

SPHINX® PUBLISHING
AN IMPRINT OF SOURCEBOOKS, INC.®
NAPERVILLE, ILLINOIS
www.SphinxLegal.com

First Edition: 2005

Published by: **Sphinx® Publishing, An Imprint of Sourcebooks, Inc.®**

Naperville Office
P.O. Box 4410
Naperville, Illinois 60567-4410
630-961-3900
Fax: 630-961-2168
www.sourcebooks.com
www.SphinxLegal.com

This publication is designed to provide accurate and authoritative information in regard to the subject matter covered. It is sold with the understanding that the publisher is not engaged in rendering legal, accounting, or other professional service. If legal advice or other expert assistance is required, the services of a competent professional person should be sought.

From a Declaration of Principles Jointly Adopted by a Committee of the
American Bar Association and a Committee of Publishers and Associations

This product is not a substitute for legal advice.

Disclaimer required by Texas statutes.

Library of Congress Cataloging-in-Publication Data
Warda, Mark.
  The complete limited liability company kit (with CD-ROM) / by Mark
Warda.-- 1st ed.
      p. cm.
  Includes index.
  ISBN-10: 1-57248-498-5 (pbk. : alk. paper)
  ISBN-13: 987-1-57248-498-6 (pbk. : alk. paper)
  1. Private companies--United States--Popular works. I. Title.

KF1380.Z9W368 2005
346.73'0668--dc22
                                                    2005009391

Printed and bound in the United States of America.
SB — 10 9 8 7 6 5

Contents

How to Use the CD-ROM

Thank you for purchasing *The Complete Limited Liability Kit (+ CD-ROM)*. An LLC provides any size business with a wealth of advantages in terms of liability protection and asset management. This book gives you exactly what you need to use those advantages to your greatest benefit. To make this material even more useful, we have included every document in the book on the CD-ROM that is attached to the inside back cover of the book.

You can use these forms just as you would the forms in the book. Print them out, fill them in, and use them however you need. You can also fill in the forms directly on your computer. Just identify the form you need, open it, click on the space where the information should go, and input your information. Customize each form for your particular needs. Use them over and over again.

The CD-ROM is compatible with both PC and Mac operating systems. (While it should work with either operating system, we cannot guarantee that it will work with your particular system and we cannot provide technical assistance.) To use the forms on your computer, you will need to use Adobe® Reader®. The CD-ROM does not contain this program. You can download this program from Adobe's website at **www.adobe.com**. Click on the "Get Adobe® Reader®" icon to begin the download process and follow the instructions.

Once you have Adobe® Reader® installed, insert the CD-ROM into your computer. Double click on the icon representing the disc on your desktop or go through your hard drive to identify the drive that contains the disc and click on it.

Once opened, you will see the files contained on the CD-ROM listed as "Form #: [Form Title]." Open the file you need through Adobe® Reader®. You may print the form to fill it out manually at this point, or your can use the "Hand Tool" and click on the appropriate line to fill it in using your computer.

Any time you see bracketed information [ ] on the form, you can click on it and delete the bracketed information from your final form. This information is only a reference guide to assist you in filling in the forms and should be removed from your final version. Once all your information is filled in, you can print your filled-in form.

NOTE: *Adobe® Reader® does not allow you to save the PDF with the boxes filled in.*

. . . .

Purchasers of this book are granted a license to use the forms contained in it for their own personal use. By purchasing this book, you have also purchased a limited license to use all forms on the accompanying CD-ROM. The license limits you to personal use only and all other copyright laws must be adhered. No claim of copyright is made in any government form reproduced in the book or on the CD-ROM. You are free to modify the forms and tailor them to your specific situation.

The author and publisher have attempted to provide the most current and up-to-date information available. However, the courts, Congress, and your state's legislatures review, modify, and change laws on an ongoing basis, as well as create new laws from time to time. By the very nature of the information and due to the continual changes in our legal system, to be sure that you have the current and best information for your situation, you should consult a local attorney or research the current laws yourself.

. . . .

This publication is designed to provide accurate and authoritative information in regard to the subject matter covered. It is sold with the understanding that the publisher is not engaged in rendering legal, accounting, or other professional service. If legal advice or other expert assistance is required, the services of a competent professional person should be sought.
    —*From a Declaration of Principles Jointly Adopted by a Committee of the American Bar Association and a Committee of Publishers and Associations*

This product is not a substitute for legal advice.
    —*Disclaimer required by Texas statutes*

Using Self-Help Law Books

Before using a self-help law book, you should realize the advantages and disadvantages of doing your own legal work and understand the challenges and diligence that this requires.

The Growing Trend

Rest assured that you won't be the first or only person handling your own legal matter. For example, in some states, more than 75% of the people in divorces and other cases represent themselves. Because of the high cost of legal services, this is a major trend and many courts are struggling to make it easier for people to represent themselves. However, some courts are not happy with people who do not use attorneys and refuse to help them in any way. For some, the attitude is, "Go to the law library and figure it out for yourself."

We write and publish self-help law books to give people an alternative to the often complicated and confusing legal books found in most law libraries. We have made the explanations of the law as simple and easy to understand as possible. Of course, unlike an attorney advising an individual client, we cannot cover every conceivable possibility.

Cost/Value Analysis

Whenever you shop for a product or service, you are faced with various levels of quality and price. In deciding what product or service to buy, you make a cost/value analysis on the basis of your willingness to pay and the quality you desire.

When buying a car, you decide whether you want transportation, comfort, status, or sex appeal. Accordingly, you decide among such choices as a Neon, a Lincoln, a Rolls Royce, or a Porsche. Before making a decision, you usually weigh the merits of each option against the cost.

When you get a headache, you can take a pain reliever (such as aspirin) or visit a medical specialist for a neurological examination. Given this choice, most people, of course, take a pain reliever, since it costs only pennies; whereas a medical examination costs hundreds of dollars and takes a lot of time. This is usually a logical choice because it is rare to need anything more than a pain reliever for a headache. But in some cases, a headache may indicate a brain tumor and failing to see a specialist right away can result in complications. Should everyone with a headache go to a specialist? Of course not, but people treating their own illnesses must realize that they are betting on the basis of their cost/value analysis of the situation. They are taking the most logical option.

The same cost/value analysis must be made when deciding to do one's own legal work. Many legal situations are very straight forward, requiring a simple form and no complicated analysis. Anyone with a little intelligence and a book of instructions can handle the matter without outside help.

But there is always the chance that complications are involved that only an attorney would notice. To simplify the law into a book like this, several legal cases often must be condensed into a single sentence or paragraph. Otherwise, the book would be several hundred pages long and too complicated for most people. However, this simplification necessarily leaves out many details and nuances that would apply to special or unusual situations. Also, there are many ways to interpret most legal questions. Your case may come before a judge who disagrees with the analysis of our authors.

Therefore, in deciding to use a self-help law book and to do your own legal work, you must realize that you are making a cost/value analysis. You have decided that the money you will save in doing it yourself outweighs the chance that your case will not turn out to your satisfaction. Most people handling their own simple legal matters never have a problem, but occasionally people find that it ended up costing them more to have an attorney straighten out the situation than it would have if they had hired an attorney in the beginning. Keep this in mind while handling your case, and be sure to consult an attorney if you feel you might need further guidance.

Local Rules

The next thing to remember is that a book which covers the law for the entire nation, or even for an entire state, cannot possibly include every procedural difference of every jurisdiction. Whenever possible, we provide the exact form needed; however, in some areas, each county, or even each judge, may require unique forms and procedures. In our state books, our forms usually cover the majority of counties in the state, or provide examples of the type of form which will be required. In our national books, our forms are sometimes even more general in nature but are designed to give a good idea of the type of form that will be needed in most locations.

Nonetheless, keep in mind that your state, county, or judge may have a requirement, or use a form, that is not included in this book.

You should not necessarily expect to be able to get all of the information and resources you need solely from within the pages of this book. This book will serve as your guide, giving you specific information whenever possible and helping you to find out what else you will need to know. This is just like if you decided to build your own backyard deck. You might purchase a book on how to build decks. However, such a book would not include the building codes and permit requirements of every city, town, county, and township in the nation; nor would it include the lumber, nails, saws, hammers, and other materials and tools you would need to actually build the deck. You would use the book as your guide, and then do some work and research involving such matters as whether you need a permit of some kind, what type and grade of wood are available in your area, whether to use hand tools or power tools, and how to use those tools.

Changes in the Law

Before using the forms in a book like this, you should check with your court clerk to see if there are any local rules of which you should be aware, or local forms you will need to use. Often, such forms will require the same information as the forms in the book but are merely laid out differently or use slightly different language. They will sometimes require additional information.

Besides being subject to local rules and practices, the law is subject to change at any time. The courts and the legislatures of all fifty states are constantly revising the laws. It is possible that while you are reading this book, some aspect of the law is being changed.

In most cases, the change will be of minimal significance. A form will be redesigned, additional information will be required, or a waiting period will be extended. As a result, you might need to revise a form, file an extra form, or wait out a longer time period; these types of changes will not usually affect the outcome of your case. On the other hand, sometimes a major part of the law is changed, the entire law in a particular area is rewritten, or a case that was the basis of a central legal point is overruled. In such instances, your entire ability to pursue your case may be impaired.

Again, you should weigh the value of your case against the cost of an attorney and make a decision as to what you believe is in your best interest.

Introduction

Each year millions of new businesses are registered throughout the country. For years *corporations* have been the preferred form of business, but the *limited liability company* is becoming more popular each year. The reason for this is that limited liability companies provide more flexibility and less paperwork than corporations, while offering nearly identical benefits.

The main reason people incorporate or form limited liability companies is to avoid personal liability for business debts and liabilities. While sole proprietors and partners are at risk of losing nearly everything they own, entrepreneurs who form an LLC or corporation risk only the *capital* they put up to start the venture. For this reason, the limited liability company is one of the few inexpensive protections left.

Before you start an LLC, review the advantages and disadvantages and the types of LLCs available. In most cases, an LLC will be better for you than other types of businesses, but in some cases, it may be more expensive or have other disadvantages. These matters are explained in Chapters 1, 2, 3, and 4.

Creating a basic limited liability company is not difficult. It is the purpose of this book to explain, in simple language, how you can do it yourself. In most states you can form your own LLC using just the forms in this book. However, in some states, special state forms may be required. These requirements have changed frequently over the years, and as explained in Chapter 5, it is best to obtain your state's latest LLC formation materials before registering your LLC. Some states provide only a short instruction sheet with no forms, but others have optional or required forms.

One document that no state provides is the *operating agreement* for the LLC. This is an important document and is explained in Chapter 5. Two different operating agreements are contained in Appendix C, to be used depending on whether your LLC will be managed by the members or by managers.

The LLC laws are not the same in every state. Each one had its own committee review the proposed law, which was subject to amendments by legislators. Therefore, a book of this kind cannot give you an exact answer to the fine details of your state's laws.

However, it can give you the general principles that apply to LLCs. Appendix A includes summaries of the main points of each state's laws. For more details, you should obtain a copy of your state's LLC statute and the formation materials provided by your secretary of state. In fact, because the statutes are amended so often, you should check the statute before filing your papers.

Some states provide free copies of the LLC statute through the secretary of state's office or through the state legislators' offices. If your state does not do this, you can photocopy the law at the library. A law library would probably have a more up-to-date statute than a public library.

Most states also have their statutes available on the Internet. You can access state laws from any of these sites:

www.findlaw.com
www.law.cornell.edu
www.alllaw.com

The limited liability company you form can be managed by the members, or it can delegate management powers to managers who are or are not members. Whenever management is delegated to managers, you should be aware of securities laws. This is explained in Chapter 6.

Chapters 7, 8, and 9 discuss the day-to-day activities of an LLC. In addition, they include explanations of raising capital, amending the original agreement, and dissolving an LLC.

A Glossary of legal terms and a section called "For Further Reference" give additional information to the reader. Appendix A lists relevant statutes—state-by-state. Appendix B contains sample, filled-in forms, and Appendix C offers blank, perforated forms for you to use.

If your situation is in any way complicated or involves factors not mentioned in this book, you should seek the advice of an attorney practicing business law. The cost of a short consultation can be a lot cheaper than the consequences of violating the law. Keep in mind, however, that the limited liability company is a special entity, and few attorneys have much experience with them. The best attorney in this type of situation is one who promotes him- or herself as practicing in this area.

This book also explains the basics of taxation, but you should discuss your own particular situation with your accountant before deciding what is best for you. He or she can also set you up with an efficient system of bookkeeping that can save both time and money.

Good luck with your new business!

Chapter 1:
What a Limited Liability Company Is

A *limited liability company* is a relatively recent invention. For hundreds of years, the three choices for a business entity were *sole proprietorship*, *partnership*, or *corporation*. However, in 1977 the LLC was invented by the state of Wyoming to fill a new need—businesses that wanted to be taxed and managed like partnerships but protected from liability like a corporation. Once the IRS accepted this arrangement, every state in the union followed suit and passed a law allowing LLCs.

The laws, however, were not identical and the effectiveness of the LLCs varied from state to state. In the beginning, single-person businesses could not use them because the law stated that a sole person could not be taxed as a partnership. However, the IRS later changed their rules to allow single-person LLCs to pass through their income to the owner.

Because the early tax laws required two or more members to avoid corporate taxation, many state laws required two persons to start an LLC. But after the tax law change, all fifty states now allow one member LLCs.

In some states there are disadvantages to using LLCs because the filing fees or annual fees are higher than for other types of businesses, such as an *S corporation*. Before forming your own LLC, you should compare the fees and requirements to be sure it offers your business the most advantages.

Legally, an LLC is a legal *person*, like a corporation, that is created under state law. As a person, an LLC has certain rights and obligations, such as the right to do business and the obligation to pay taxes. (Sometimes one hears of a law referring to *natural persons*. That is to differentiate natural persons from corporations and LLCs, which, as stated earlier, are considered persons, but not natural persons.)

Limited Personal Risk

The idea behind both the LLC and the corporation is to allow people to invest in a new business but not risk unlimited personal liability. Before the corporation was invented hundreds of years ago, people who invested in, say, an expedition to the New World to look for gold, could lose everything they owned in the event the venture went into debt. The invention of the corporation allowed people to put a limited sum of money into such a venture, split the profits if it succeeded, and not be liable for more if it failed.

The reasons for having a corporation or LLC are the same today. They allow investors to put up money for new ventures without risk of further liability. However, before forming an LLC, you should be familiar with the following common terms that will be used in the text.

Member

A *member* is a person who owns an interest in a limited liability company, similar to the stockholder of a corporation. In an LLC the members have the option of running the company themselves or having managers who are or are not members. Until recently, some states required an LLC to have two or more members; but now that the IRS allows favorable tax treatment for one-member LLCs, the states are changing their laws to allow them.

Manager

A *manager* is someone who runs the affairs of an LLC. In most states an LLC can be either managed by all the members equally, or it can have a manager or managers who may or may not be members.

Managing Member

A managing member is a member of the LLC who runs the operations. If all of the members do not want to manage the LLC, then one or more of them can be designated managing member.

Registered Agent and Registered Office

The *registered agent* is the person designated by a limited liability company to receive legal papers that must be served on the company. (In a few states the term *statutory agent* is used.) The registered agent should be regularly available at the registered office of the corporation. The *registered office* can be the company offices or the office of the company's attorney, or whomever is the registered agent. At the time of registration, some states require the company to file a Certificate of Designation of Registered Agent/Registered Office. This contains a statement that must be signed by the registered agent that he or she understands the duties and responsibilities of the position.

Articles of Organization

Articles of Organization is the document that is filed to start the limited liability company. (In a few states, it may have a slightly different name, such as *Certificate of Organization.*) In most cases it only needs to contain a few basic statements. More provisions can be added, but usually it is better to put such provisions in the membership agreement rather than the articles because amendment of the latter is more complicated.

Operating Agreement

The *operating agreement* is the document that sets out rights and obligations of the members and the rules for running the company. An operating agreement is not required in every state, but having one is a good idea. If such an agreement has not been signed by the members, the rules provided in your state's statute apply.

Membership Operating Agreement

If the LLC is run by its members, the agreement is usually called a *membership operating agreement.* Even if the LLC has only one member, it is important to have an operating agreement to spell out the nonliability of the member for debts of the company.

Management Operating Agreement

If the LLC is to be managed by less than all the members, or by someone who is not a member, there should be a management agreement spelling out the rights and duties of the members and the managers. This can be combined into the operating agreement, in which case it would be called a *management operating agreement.*

Annual Report

Most states require some sort of annual report to keep the state updated on the members and status of the company. In most cases, the company will be dissolved if this form is not filed on time, and in some states, there is a very high fee to reinstate the company.

Other Forms

Some states require various other forms to establish an LLC. These will be mentioned in Appendix A or in materials you may receive from your state.

Chapter 2:
Advantages and
Disadvantages of an LLC

Before forming a limited liability company, the business owner or prospective business owner should become familiar with the advantages and disadvantages of the LLC and how they compare to those of other business entities.

Compared to Proprietorships and Partnerships

The limited liability company offers the greatest benefits when compared to *partnerships* and *sole proprietorships*. Now that the LLC structure is available, it is advisable for most partnerships and sole proprietorships to switch.

Advantages

There are several advantages to having your business be an LLC. This section describes some of those advantages and how to apply them to certain situations.

Limited Liability

The main reason for forming a limited liability company or corporation is to limit the liability of the owners. In a sole proprietorship or partnership, the owners are personally liable for the debts and liabilities of the business, and creditors can go after nearly all of their assets to collect. If an LLC is formed and operated properly, the owners can be protected from all such liability.

Example 1: *If several people are in a partnership and one of them makes many large, extravagant purchases in the name of the partnership, the other partners can be liable for the full amount of all such purchases. The creditors can take the bank accounts, cars, real estate, and other property of any partner to pay the debts of the partnership. If only one partner has money, he or she may have* *to pay all of the debts accumulated by the other partners. When doing business in the LLC or corporate form, the business may go bankrupt and the shareholders may lose their initial investment, but the creditors cannot touch the personal assets of the owners.*

Example 2: *If an employee of a partnership causes a terrible accident, the partnership and all the partners can be held personally liable for millions of dollars in damages. With a corporation or LLC, only the business would be liable whether or not there was enough money to cover the damages.*

One true story involves a business owner who owned hundreds of taxis. He put one or two in each of hundreds of different corporations that he owned. Each corporation only had minimum insurance and when one taxi was involved in an accident, the owner only lost the assets of that corporation. The injured party tried to reach the owner's other assets, but the court ruled that this was a valid use of the corporate structure.

Note: *If a member of a limited liability company does something negligent, signs a debt personally, or guarantees a company debt, the limited liability company will not protect him or her from the consequences of his or her own act or from the debt. Also, if a limited liability company fails to follow proper formalities, a court may use that as an excuse to hold the members liable. The formalities include having separate bank accounts, filing annual reports, and following other requirements of state law.*

Since the limited liability company is relatively new, there have been few cases interpreting the law. Courts will most likely look to both corporation and partnership law when ruling in a limited liability company case. When a court ignores a corporate structure and holds the owners or officers liable, it is called *piercing the corporate veil.* (It is not yet clear how or when the courts would allow a party to pierce the LLC structure.) Aspects of asset protection for an LLC are explained in more detail in Chapter 4.

Continuous Existence

A limited liability company may have a perpetual existence. When a sole proprietor dies, the assets of his or her business may pass to the heirs but the business no longer exists. (This may also happen with a partnership if it is not set up right.) If the surviving spouse or other heirs of a business owner want to continue the business in their own names, they will be considered a new business—even if they are using the assets of the old business. With a partnership, the death of one partner can cause a *dissolution* of the business if there is no provision in the partnership agreement for it to continue.

Example: *If the owner of a sole proprietorship dies, his or her spouse may want to continue the business. That person may inherit all of the assets, but would have to
start a new business. This means getting new licenses and tax numbers, registering the name, and establishing credit from scratch. With an LLC, the business
continues with all of the same licenses, bank accounts, and so on.*

Ease of Transferability

A limited liability company and all of its assets and accounts may be transferred by the simple
transfer of interest in the company. With a sole proprietorship, each of the individual assets must
be transferred and the accounts, licenses, and permits must be individually transferred.

Example: *If a sole proprietorship is sold, the new owner will have to get a new occupational license, set up his or her own bank account, and apply for a new taxpayer
identification number. The title to any vehicles or real estate will have to be put
in his or her name, and all open accounts will have to be changed to his or her
name. He or she will probably have to submit new credit applications. With an
LLC or corporation, all of these items remain in the same business name and
are under control of the new manager or officer.*

Note: *In some cases, the new owners will have to submit personal applications for such things as
credit lines or liquor licenses.*

Sharing Ownership

With a limited liability company, the owner of a business can share the profits of a business without giving up control. This is done by setting up the share of profits separate from the share of
ownership.

Example: *John wants to give his children some of the profits of his business. He can make
them members of the company entitled to a share of the profits without giving
them any control over the management. This would not be practical with a
partnership or sole proprietorship.*

Ease of Raising Capital

A limited liability company may raise capital by admitting new members or borrowing money.
In most cases, a business does not pay taxes on money it raises through the sale of its shares.

Example: *If an LLC or corporation wants to expand, the owners can sell 10%, 50%, or
90% of the ownership and still remain in control of the business. The people
putting up the money may be more willing to invest if they know they will have*

a piece of the action than if they were making a loan with a limited return. They may not want to become partners in a partnership.

Note: *There are strict rules about selling interests in businesses with criminal penalties and triple damages for violators. (see Chapter 5.)*

Separate Record Keeping
An LLC has all its own bank accounts and records. A sole proprietor may have trouble differentiating which expenses were for business and which were for personal items.

Ease of Estate Planning
With an LLC or corporation, shares of a company can be distributed more easily than with a partnership or sole proprietorship. Different heirs can be given different percentages, and control can be limited to those who are most capable.

Prestige
The name of an LLC or corporation sounds more prestigious than the name of a sole proprietor to some people. John Smith d/b/a Acme Builders sounds like one lone guy. Acme Builders, L.L.C., sounds like it might be a large sophisticated operation. One female writer on the subject has suggested that a woman who is president of a corporation looks more successful than a woman doing business in her own name. This would be the same with an LLC and would apply to everyone.

Separate Credit Rating
An LLC has its own credit rating, which can be better or worse than the owner's credit rating. An LLC can go bankrupt while the owner's credit remains unaffected, or an owner's credit may be bad, but the corporation may maintain a good rating.

Disadvantages
The main disadvantage that most professionals see in the LLC is that the law is new and it is not yet known how the courts will interpret it. But for some lawyers this is an excuse not to learn new things. It is always more comfortable to do what you have always done. But while there is always a chance for bad interpretation of the law, most cases should turn out as the law intended, and owners of LLCs should be protected from liability.

Cost
Compared to a sole proprietorship or partnership, an LLC is more expensive to operate. In some states the fees are as low as $50 or even $10, but in others they are hundreds of dollars each year. However, this cost is offset by the lesser need for liability insurance.

Separate Records

The owners of a limited liability company must be careful to keep their personal business separate from the business of the limited liability company. The limited liability company must have its own records and should have minutes of meetings. Money must be kept separate. Records should be separate in every business and the structure of a company might make it easier to do so.

Taxes

A limited liability company owner will have to pay *unemployment compensation tax* for him- or herself, which he or she would not have to pay as a sole proprietor.

Banking

Checks made out to a limited liability company cannot be cashed; they must be deposited into a corporate account. Some banks have higher fees just for businesses that are incorporated. (See pages 34–35 for tips on avoiding high bank fees.)

Compared to Limited Partnerships

A *limited partnership* is an entity in which one or more partners control the business and are liable for the debts (the *general partners*), and one or more partners have no say in the business nor liability for the debts (the *limited partners*). This is expensive to set up because the limited partnership agreement is costly.

The limited liability company allows a similar structure at a lower cost with the added benefit that no one needs to be liable for the debts of the business. For most businesses that were once limited partnerships, the LLC is now the preferred form of business.

Compared to Corporations

The biggest advantage of an LLC over a corporation is that in most states it provides double asset protection. A corporation provides asset protection in that a shareholder is protected from liabilities of the corporation. But a member of an LLC gets this protection, plus personal creditors cannot take his or her LLC away from him or her if set up correctly. This is explained in more detail in the next chapter.

- ◆ An LLC requires less formality than a corporation. While improper procedures in a corporation may allow a creditor to *pierce the corporate veil* and hold shareholders liable, the LLC is meant to be a safe harbor to protect business owners from liability.
- ◆ An LLC can make special allocations of profits and losses among members, whereas an S corporation cannot. S corporations must have one class of ownership in which profits and losses are allocated according to the percentage of ownership.

◆ In an LLC, money borrowed by the company can increase the *tax basis* of the owners (and lower the taxes); whereas in an S corporation, it does not.

◆ Contributing property to set up an LLC is not taxable even for minority interest owners. In the case of a corporation, the Internal Revenue Code Section 351 only allows it to be tax free for the contributors who have control of the business.

◆ The owners of an LLC can be foreign persons, other corporations, or any kind of trust. This is not true for the owners of S corporations.

◆ An LLC may have an unlimited number of members while an S corporation is limited to one hundred.

◆ If an S corporation violates one of the rules, it can lose its S corporation status and not be allowed to regain it for five years.

NOTE: *Another advantage may be psychological. The LLC is still a relatively new entity, and in the twenty-first century it may look more up-to-date to be an LLC rather than an ordinary corporation.*

The main disadvantage of an LLC, which is taxed as a disregarded entity compared to an S corporation, is that with an S corporation, profits taken out other than salary are not subject to social security and medicare taxes (15.3% at the time of publication); whereas all profits of an LLC are subject to these taxes (up to the taxable limits). However, if this is an issue for you, you can opt to have your LLC taxed as a corporation and then choose S corporation status. (see Chapter 4.)

For a large business where the owners take out salaries of $80,000 or more plus profits, there would not be much difference since the social security tax does not apply above that level. But for a smaller business where an owner would take out, say, $30,000 salary and $20,000 profit, the extra taxes would be over $3,000.

In some states, a disadvantage of an LLC is its start-up and annual fees are higher than for an S corporation.

Converting an Existing Business

While an LLC may appear to be the best type of business entity for you, if you have an existing business, you should weigh the time and expense involved in making the conversion.

A sole proprietorship would be the easiest to convert, and a corporation would be the most complicated. (The corporation has potential tax issues which should be reviewed by a tax specialist.) At a minimum, some of the things which will have to be handled in your conversion are federal employer identification number, state tax account numbers, fictitious name registration, business licenses, professional licenses (if any), bank accounts, vendor accounts, customer accounts, and utilities.

Business Comparison Chart

	SOLE PROPRIETORSHIP	GENERAL PARTNERSHIP	LIMITED PARTNERSHIP	LIMITED LIABILITY CO.	CORPORATION C OR S	NONPROFIT CORPORATION
Liability Protection	No	No	For limited partners	For all members	For all shareholders	For all members
Taxes	Pass through	Pass through	Pass through	Pass through or LLC can pay	S corps. pass through C corps. pay tax	None on income— Employees pay on wages
Minimum # of members	1	2	2	1	1	1 to 3
Diff. classes of ownership	No	Yes	Yes	Yes	S corps.–No C corps.–Yes	No ownership— Different classes of membership
Survives after Death	No	No	Yes	Yes	Yes	Yes
Best for	1 person, low-risk business or no assets	Low-risk business	Low-risk business with silent partners	All types of businesses	All types of businesses	Educational

Chapter 3:
Types of LLCs

Before forming your LLC, you need to decide which type of limited liability company it will be. There are several choices to choose from, each based on your particular circumstance.

Domestic LLC or Foreign LLC

A person wishing to form a limited liability company must decide whether the company will be a *domestic* LLC or a *foreign* LLC. For our purposes, a domestic LLC is one you form in the state in which you do business, and a foreign LLC is one you form in another state to do business in your state.

Delaware LLCs

In the past, there was an advantage to forming a business in Delaware, because of its liberal business laws and a long history of court decisions favorable to businesses. Many national corporations were formed there for that reason. However, most states have liberalized their business laws over the years. Today, in most cases, there is no advantage to forming a business in Delaware unless you are doing business there.

This would be an advantage in states with high LLC fees or high personal income tax. If the sole purpose of your LLC was to own a piece of property (as opposed to running a business), you could take advantage of Delaware's lower fees. But be sure to check your state's definition of doing business to make sure your activities are outside of it; otherwise, you will end up paying double fees—your state's full fees plus Delaware's.

To save on income taxes, you could form a Delaware company that would siphon profits away from your local company, for example, by providing consulting services out of state. The money paid would avoid your state income tax and Delaware does not have an income tax on LLCs. (You would not avoid federal income taxes, only your state's income tax.)

Nevada LLCs

Nevada has liberalized its business laws recently to attract more companies. It allows more privacy and other benefits depending on the type of entity. It does not have a state income tax, nor does it share information with the Internal Revenue Service. If you are concerned about privacy, you should review the Nevada information page in Appendix A and compare the costs to those in your own state. If your state has high LLC fees or a state income tax, the benefits described for a Delaware LLC would also apply to Nevada.

Disadvantage

The biggest disadvantage to forming a business in Nevada, Delaware, or any state other than the one you are in, is you will need to have an agent or an office in that state and will have to register as a foreign corporation doing business in your state. This is more expensive and more complicated than registering in your own state. You can also be sued in the state in which your company was formed. This would be more expensive for you to defend than a suit filed in your local court. Additionally, if you incorporate in a state which has an income tax, you may have to pay taxes there even if you only do business in your own state.

Membership Controlled or Management Controlled

The next thing you will need to decide is whether your LLC will be membership controlled or management controlled. If the LLC is being formed by one person or a small group of people who will all operate it as partners, you should designate it as membership controlled and execute a *membership operating agreement*. If the LLC will have silent partners and be managed by other members or nonmembers, you should designate it management controlled and execute a *management operating agreement*. These documents are explained in Chapter 6 and are included in Appendix C.

LLC or PLLC

In many states, professionals such as lawyers, doctors, veterinarians, architects, life insurance agents, chiropractors, and accountants are allowed to set up LLCs. These are designated *PLLCs* or something of a similar nature.

Again, since the laws covering professional LLCs are state laws, you will need to get a copy of your state's statute to be sure your plan complies with all of the requirements. You should also check with the *licensing board* that regulates your profession to see if they impose any additional requirements on professional LLCs. In some states, professionals may be required to obtain malpractice insurance if they form a PLLC.

Following are some of the other types of rules that may apply to professional LLCs.

- The professional limited liability company must have one specific purpose spelled out in the Articles of Organization, and the purpose must be to practice one of the professions. Usually the PLLC may not engage in any other business, but it may invest its funds in real estate, stocks, bonds, mortgages, or other types of investments.
- The name of the professional service corporation must contain the word "chartered" or "professional limited company" or the abbreviation "PLLC."
- Only persons licensed to practice the profession may be members of a professional service limited liability company, and a member who loses his or her right to practice must immediately sever all employment with and financial interests in the company.
- A professional service limited liability company may not merge with any other limited liability company except another professional service corporation that is licensed to perform the same type of services.

Single-Member or Multiple-Member

Whether you use a single-member or multiple-member LLC is not just a function of the number of people involved. Because of the advantages and disadvantages of each, a single business owner might want to form a multiple-member company and multiple people might want to form single-member companies.

For example, a person with a one-person business who wants to start a multiple-member LLC to gain asset protection, might want to make his spouse, parent, or child a member. Two people who own lots of properties as separate LLCs might want to make them single-member LLCs owned by one multiple-member LLC to avoid filing a separate tax return for each. (See chart on page 20 for a breakdown of tax returns filed.)

You will have an operating agreement whether you are single- or multiple-member company. But for a multiple-member company, you need to be more careful to spell out each others' rights in the event of a split-up, death, or irreconcilable disagreement.

Taxes

A single-member LLC is easier for tax purposes because no tax return is required. The income is reported on the member's tax return. A multiple member LLC must file IRS Form 1065, file the partnership tax return, and give the members K-1 forms to file with their returns. If you do your own taxes, this may be just another form to file, but if you have a professional tax preparer, it may cost hundreds of dollars. If you set up numerous LLCs, this can get expensive.

Asset Protection

While a single-member LLC is simpler for tax purposes, it probably will not be allowed double asset protection. You need two or more members for the double asset protection that an LLC offers. Therefore, if your LLC will have substantial assets, it should be set up as multiple-member to obtain asset protection.

Chapter 4:
Asset Protection

The main reason for having an LLC is to limit liability. Because the asset protection advantages of an LLC are so much greater than other entities, this chapter explains them in detail.

Double Asset Protection

The really great thing about the LLC is that it offers two types of asset protection. One is the same as a corporation; the other is the same as a limited partnership. Together these make the LLC one of the most valuable asset protection tools that exist.

Corporate-Type Protection

A corporation protects its owners from liability in that the shareholders are protected from the debts and liabilities of the business. If you own stock in General Motors, you will not be liable if they default on their bonds or if someone sues General Motors for defective cars and wins billions of dollars.

This same type of protection is available to you if you own a corporation (S corporation or C corporation) or an LLC. If the company is liable for something (and you did not personally cause it) then you as the shareholder or member will in most cases not be liable.

Limited Partnership-Type Protection

In most states an LLC provides an additional type of asset protection, protection of your LLC interest from your personal creditors. This means that if you do something personally that makes you liable, for example you get into an auto accident, the creditor cannot take your LLC assets away from you. What the law says is that your creditor can only get a *charging order* against your interest. This means that it has to pay taxes on the income of the LLC, but that it cannot get any money out of the LLC unless the other LLC members decide to give it. Needless to say, most creditors do not even want charging orders.

Any assets you put into an LLC can be safe from your personal creditors, no matter what you do—malpractice, auto accidents, divorce, bankruptcy, etc. But note the word *can*. In law nothing is black and white, and new law is an especially gray area. If you follow the rules, however, you can be successful.

Requirements for Double Asset Protection

While the law says that a creditor can only have a charging order against an LLC interest, at least one court has ruled that if the LLC has only one member, the creditor can take the company. The rationale was that the charging order rule was designed to protect other members of a business from disruption from one member's creditors, and this does not make sense in a one-member company. So you need at least two members of your LLC to get the double asset protection.

Entrepreneurs who do not really want someone else in their business look for ways to have a two-member company, but to still keep full control. Some of the suggestions have been to have part of the LLC owned by:

   ◆ a corporation owned by the member;
   ◆ another LLC owned by the member;
   ◆ a trust owned by the member;
   ◆ a child; or,
   ◆ a parent.

Will these work? If the one member really controls 100%, then probably not. Courts usually look to the substance of the whole transaction to see what the reality is. If you just assign 2% of your LLC to your corporation solely to avoid creditors, it will probably be considered a sham transaction.

What would work would be a setup with some purpose. If your parent made a small investment in your business in exchange for a small percentage of ownership, that would be legitimate. If you set up a trust for your children's education, and it bought a part of your LLC, that would probably also be seen as legitimate.

Example: *One doctor sold a small percentage of his LLC to his accountant. If this appeared to be a plan to share profits in exchange for services, rather than merely a sham, it might work.*

One thing to consider is that the success of a plan depends on the sophistication of the creditor. A thorough examination by a sophisticated creditor's attorney could make any plan look suspect; however, if a new attorney is faced with multiple LLCs and a complicated setup that could take months to decipher, he or she might be willing to accept your settlement offer or insurance limits rather than spend the time to try to get through it.

The fact that this is a gray area of law works two ways. For the person wanting the protection, it does not give clear answers on what works best. But for the creditor, it does not provide how to win. No matter what type of LLC arrangement you have set up, if a creditor wins against you, you can appeal it and argue that the law gives you more protection. Plaintiff's lawyers do not like to spend years in court unless there is a significant payoff. A small business with a complicated structure and no sure legal basis would be a good candidate for a quick settlement.

When to Use a Single-Member Company

While a single-member LLC does not provide double asset protection, it can still be very useful in many situations. Remember, a single-member LLC protects the owner against business claims but does not protect the business from the member's creditors. So the best use occurs when the business would have claims, but the company does not have many assets worth claiming.

A good example is a property management company. Many real estate investors have one LLC set up to manage their properties. Usually it will collect the rents and pay the mortgages and expenses of the properties. This company deals with the tenants and has a high risk of getting sued. But if it spends all the money it collects in rents, it will not have many assets so it does not need double asset protection.

Another use could be to own individual properties. If you have one LLC that owns five properties then a liability on one of them could cause you to lose them all. A better plan would be to have each property in a separate single-member LLC all owned by one multiple-member LLC. The single-member LLCs would not file tax returns but would pass through their income to the multiple-member LLC. (*Thanks to David Burton, CPA, of Harper Van Skoik & Co., Clearwater, FL, for this planning.*)

The chart on page 20 demonstrates how multiple LLCs can be used to hold investments, as well as when tax returns would need to be filed, based on whether it was a single-member company or a multiple-member LLC.

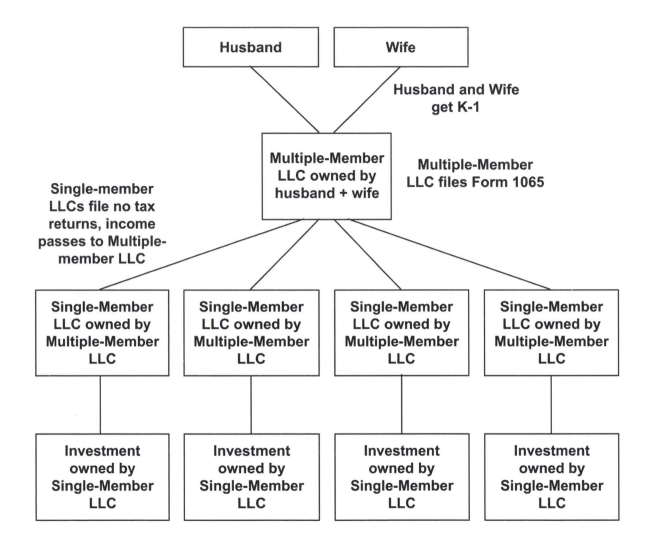

Chapter 5:
Start-Up Procedures

This chapter explains the steps you need to follow in setting up your LLC.

Choosing the Company Name

The very first thing to do before starting a limited liability company is to thoroughly research the name you wish to use to be sure it is available. Many businesses have been forced to stop using their name after spending thousands of dollars promoting it.

Local Records

To check for other businesses in your state using a certain name, you can call or write your secretary of state's office, or in some states, you can do your own search using their website. The phone number, address, and website address for your state (if applicable) is on the state page in Appendix A. If your name is too similar to another company's name, you will not be allowed to register it.

You should also ask about *fictitious* or *assumed names*. In some states, these are registered with the secretary of state and in others, with the county recorder or court office. In some states, the secretary of state does not limit the number of people who may register the same name. An infringement would depend upon whether they used the name in the same area.

Business Listings

Since some businesses neglect to properly register their name (yet still may have superior rights to the name), you should also check phone books and business directories. Many libraries have phone books from around the country, as well as directories of trade names.

Federal Trademarks

It is possible to use a name similar to the names of businesses elsewhere in the country without problems, but if they have registered a federal trademark of the name, they can force you to stop using it, and you could be liable for damages. It is best to check the trademarks registered with the United States Patent and Trademark Office.

Trademark Records Search

Up until 1999, the only ways to search the records of the United States Patent and Trademark Office were to go there, use a Trademark Depository Library, or hire a search firm to do a search. But now you can do a search instantly on the Internet. The website is www.uspto.gov. Once there click on "Search" under "Trademarks" on the left side of the screen. Here is what you will see:

The database is updated regularly, but it is usually a few weeks behind schedule. You will see the date it is current through in the first paragraph. Clicking on the "News!" button will give you the latest complete filing date available online from the USPTO. As a practical matter, if a mark you are considering has not been registered in the last two hundred years, it is not likely that it has been in the last few weeks, but it is possible, especially if you are using a mark related to the latest technology. If you wish to update your mark through the latest filings, you will need to either visit the USPTO or hire a search firm to do so.

The USPTO records are not completely up-to-date and without experience at searching them you might miss a trademark. You might want to hire a professional search company to give you a written report. Some firms that do searches are:

Government Liaison Services, Inc.
200 North Glebe Road, Suite 321
Arlington, VA 22203
800-642-6564
www.trademarkinfo.com

Thomson & Thomson
500 Victory Road
North Quincy, MA 02171-3145
800-692-8833
www.thomson-thomson.com

XL Corporate Service
62 White Street
New York, NY 10013-3593
212-431-5000

Similar Names

Sometimes it seems like every good name is taken. But a name can often be modified slightly or used for a different type of goods or services. If there is a "TriCounty Painting, L.L.C." in another part of your state, it may be possible to use something such as "TriCounty Painting of Libertyville, L.L.C." if you are in a different part of the state. Try different variations if your favorite is taken. Keep in mind that if you eventually expand your business to an area where the name is being used, you can be barred from using it in that area. In such a case, you would be better off using a completely different name.

Another possibility is to give the corporation one name and do business under a fictitious name. (See "Fictitious or Assumed Names" on page 25.)

Example: *If you want to use the name "Flowers by Freida" in your city and there is already a "Flowers by Freida, Inc." in another part of the state, you might register your company under the name "Freida Jones, L.L.C." and register the company as doing business under the fictitious name "Flowers by Freida." Unless "Flowers by Freida, Inc." has registered a state or federal trademark for the name, you will probably be able to use the name.*

Note: *You should realize that you might run into complications later, especially if you decide to expand into other areas of the state. One protection available would be to register the name as a* *trademark. This would give you exclusive use of the name anywhere that someone else was not already using it.*

Name Requirements

There are requirements that the limited liability company name contain wording indicating that it is a limited liability company. Depending on the state, it may require one or all of the following:

L.C.	LC	limited company
L.L.C.	LLC	limited liability company

In some states you can use just the word "limited" or the abbreviation "ltd." Be sure to check your state rules before making a choice.

The name cannot include any words implying that it is part of the state or federal government or that it is in any business in which it is not authorized to be.

In some states, professional LLCs must also use certain words, such as "chartered" or "professional limited liability company." Again, the specific state rule must be checked.

Forbidden Names

A limited liability company may not use certain words in its name if there would be a likelihood of confusion. There are state and federal laws that control the use of these words. In most cases, your application will be rejected if you use a forbidden word. Some of the words that may not be used without special licenses or registration are:

Assurance	Insurance
Banc	Lottery
Bank	Olympiad
Banker	Olympic
Banking	Savings Bank
College	Savings and Loan Association
Cooperative	Trust Company
Credit Union	University
Disney	

Trademarks

The name of a business cannot be registered as a trademark, unless the name is used in connection with goods and services. In that case, it may be registered and such registration will grant the holder exclusive rights to use that name except in areas where someone else has already used the name. A trademark may be registered either in each state or in the United States Patent and Trademark Office which covers the entire country.

Each trademark is registered for a certain "class" of goods. If you want to sell "Zapata" chewing gum, it does not matter that someone has registered the name "Zapata" for use in another category, such as shoes. (An exception to this rule is where a trademark has become famous. For example, even though Coca-Cola is a trademark for a beverage, you could not use the name Coca-Cola for chewing gum.) If you want to register the mark for several types of goods or services, you must register it for each different class into which the goods or services fall, and pay a separate fee for each category.

Every state has a procedure for registering a trademark for statewide protection. This protects a mark throughout the state from anyone who might want to use the same mark in the future, but does not affect the rights of people who already use the mark in the state. It also does not stop people in other states from using the mark. The form is simple and the cost is minimal in most states. For more information, phone, write, or check the website of your secretary of state.

For protection across the entire United States, the mark can be registered with the United States Patent and Trademark Office for a fee of $325 if filed online, or $375 if paper filed. The procedure for federal registration is more complicated than state registration. You can find some information and forms on the website of the United States Patent and Trademark Office:

www.uspto.gov

Unregistered Names

Even if a business does not register its name, it still has legal rights to it. Therefore, you should check to see if any other businesses have the name you intend to use. If a business in your area has a similar name, you should not use it. If the business is farther away, you can use it if you do not expect to do business in that area, but a completely different name is still better.

For a thorough search, you can use the Internet search engines Google or Yahoo, but you may find more listings than you can ever look at. (For example, a search of "Sphinx" returns over a million references.) If you go to a White Pages listing of business names you will get a more limited list. One site that lets you search all states at once is **www.switchboard.com**.

Fictitious or Assumed Names

The name of an LLC is its legal name. However, it can also operate under a *fictitious name* (called an *assumed name* in some states) just as an individual can. This is done when a company wants to operate several businesses under different names or if the business name is not available as a company name.

Example: *An LLC may have the legal name Elizabeth Bartlett, LLC, and open a bakery called "Betty B's Breads & Buns."*

Registration of a fictitious name is either done with the secretary of state or a county recorder. Check with the office in your area for forms and instructions.

Note: *When a fictitious name is used by a limited liability company, the company's legal name should also be used in conjunction with it whenever possible. If the public does not see that they are dealing with a limited liability company, they may be able to use the same theory of piercing the corporate veil to collect against the members individually.*

State LLC Laws and Forms

Each state has adopted its own version of the statute allowing LLCs, so each state will have slightly different requirements as to what the filing documents must contain. Also, not every state will supply the same materials. Some send only a single page of vague instructions, while others send a large packet including a copy of the statute and numerous forms.

If your state provides a form, using that form may speed up your proceedings. Some states provide the form in downloadable format on the Internet, and others only use the mail. (If you have access to the Internet, you can check the site for your state listed in Appendix A.)

California appears to be the only state which requires that its own form be used. Others allow people to draft their own articles as long as all the required information is included. (The California form is included in Appendix A.)

If your state does not provide a form, or if you wish to get started without waiting for the form, you can use the blank form in this book or retype the information yourself. The good thing about forming an LLC is that if you make a mistake, such as forgetting a required provision, the filing office will usually return it for correction rather than let you file it wrong and have a defective company.

One form which no state supplies is the *operating agreement*. (This is explained later in this chapter and blank forms are included in Appendix C.)

Summaries of the state *statutes* are included in Appendix A, but because the laws are new, they are fine tuned every year or two. Your state's laws may have changed by the time you read this. You can get the statutes for most states on the Internet. (See the Introduction to this book for sites.) If you do not have access to the Internet, you may be able to obtain a copy from your secretary of state or your state legislator, or photocopy it at the library.

When getting a copy of your state statute, find out the date it was last updated and when your state legislature convenes. If a session recently ended, there may be changes to the law that are not included in your copy of the statute. A librarian at a law library would be most knowledgeable as to which copy of the statute is most up-to-date.

Once you get a copy of the laws, you should become familiar with the filing and operational requirements for LLCs. General rules are included in this book, but some states have some more specific requirements. Do not be intimidated if the statute is long. Many of the provisions will apply to *mergers* or *dissolutions,* which do not concern you at this point.

Articles of Organization

The action that creates the limited liability company in most states is the filing of Articles of Organization with the secretary of state. In a few states there may be another filing office or the document may have a slightly different name. (Some states require additional forms to complete the registration as explained on page 30.)

Usual Requirements

Requirements for the articles of organization are listed below. Some states require an extra clause or two, which is discussed in the next section.

Name

The name must include the suffix (LLC, LC, etc.).

Purpose

Many states require that the business purpose be stated, though this may be stated as "any lawful purpose for which limited liability companies may be formed." A few states ask for a specific *industry code.*

Period of Duration

This may be stated as perpetual in most states. In Utah, it cannot exceed ninety-nine years, and in Nebraska and South Dakota, it cannot exceed thirty years.

Name and Street Address of the Initial Registered (or Statutory) agent

In many states, the registered agent also must sign a form stating that he or she is familiar with and accepts the obligations of the position.

Each limited liability company must have a *registered agent* and a *registered office*. The registered agent can be any individual or a corporation. The registered office can be the business office of the limited liability company if the registered agent works out of that office, or it can be the office of another individual who is the registered agent (such as an attorney) or a corporate registered agent's office. The business address of the registered agent is considered the registered office of the limited liability company. In most LLCs, one of the members is the registered agent at the business address. Technically, it may not be a residence unless that address is also a business office of the limited liability company.

Management

Must state whether the company will be managed by the members or by separate managers. In most states, all of their names and addresses must be included, whether or not they are members or separate managers.

Principle Place of Business

This must be a street address in most states, but a mailing address can also be included.

Effective Date

Many states want to know the effective date of the articles. Usually, this is the date of filing.

Nonliability

Five states (Hawaii, South Carolina, South Dakota, Vermont, and West Virginia) require a statement of whether the members are liable for the debts of the company. Several other states say that a clause can be added stating whether the members are liable. Since the main purpose of forming an LLC is to avoid personal liability, we have included a nonliability clause in the Articles in this book. If using a state form, you should not check any box stating that the members are liable.

It is best to keep your Articles to the bare legal minimum and put any other *provisions* in the operating agreement. This is because it is much easier to amend the operating agreement than the Articles if you want to make changes at a later date.

Additional Clauses

The following clauses are sometimes put into LLC Articles. In some states, one or more of these clauses may be required. (See your state page in Appendix A for "Articles Special Requirements.")

The Right, If Any, to Admit New Members

If the LLC will allow new members to be admitted, there must be a clause stating so. Some states require this to be in the articles along with the terms and conditions of admission. Here is some sample language:

> New members can be admitted to the company with full rights of membership upon the unanimous consent of the existing members.

Members' Rights to Continue Business

This clause states whether the remaining members can continue the business after the death, retirement, resignation, expulsion, bankruptcy, dissolution of a member, or any other event that terminates membership. Some states require that this be spelled out. Here is a sample clause:

> The company can continue the business after the death, retirement, resignation, expulsion, bankruptcy, or dissolution of a member, or any other event that terminates membership, upon the unanimous consent of the remaining members.

Organizers

In some cases, the organizers of the company are different from the members (such as if an attorney or paralegal files the papers). Colorado, the District of Columbia, Illinois, and Oregon require that the organizers be disclosed in the articles.

Professional LLCs

In most states there is a separate portion of the statutes that govern "professional LLCs" and other professional companies. This contains specific requirements that these entities must follow. Some typical things that the statute may require are:

- ◆ the business purpose is limited to the practice of the one profession for which it was organized;
- ◆ no person or entity can be admitted as a member unless he, she, or it is qualified to practice the profession, and no interest can be sold except to someone so qualified; and,
- ◆ some states require members of professional LLCs to carry certain limits of malpractice insurance.

If forming a professional LLC, you should obtain a copy of the statute that governs them in your state. Also, check with the board that regulates your profession—they may have additional regulations that apply. If they do not provide a form, you can use the form included in this book, adding the necessary clauses to "Article IX–Miscellaneous" or retyping the Articles if there is not enough room. Typically, the additional clauses would be worded like this:

No person may be admitted to membership who is not licensed to practice _____ in this state. No interest in this company may be sold to anyone who is not so licensed. Any member whose license to practice is revoked or terminated shall immediately terminate his or her membership.

Additional Forms

Some states require forms to be filed in addition to the articles of organization. The following states require the forms listed. These requirements may change, so check with your state for additional requirements.

Arizona	Affidavit of Publication
Arkansas	Franchise Tax Registration Form
California	Tax Voucher (form 3522)
Washington D.C.	Consent of Registered Agent
Florida	*Certificate of Designation of Registered Agent
Georgia	Transmittal Form 231
Louisiana	Initial Report
Maine	*Acceptance of Appointment as Registered Agent
Michigan	If Form C&S 700 is not used for your articles, it must accompany your articles.
New Hampshire	Addendum to Certificate of Formation
New York	Affidavit of Publication
North Dakota	Registered Agent Consent to Serve
Ohio	Original Appointment of Agent
Pennsylvania	Docketing Statement DSCB: 15-134A
South Dakota	First Annual Report
Wyoming	Consent to Appointment of Registered Agent

*The information on these forms can be incorporated into the articles, in which case the separate form does not need to be filed.

Execution and Filing

Some states allow any person to sign an LLC's articles of organization (even an agent or attorney), but others require a member or all the members to sign. (Check the page for your state in Appendix A.) To avoid delay in case your state's rules have changed, you can have all members sign even if it does not appear that it is required.

Some states require the form to be signed in black ink, but it is advisable for everyone to do so in case your state recently adopted the requirement. Most also require typing or printing.

Some states return the form quickly, while others normally take several weeks but will file it quicker for an additional charge. Some provide a street address for courier service (FedEx, Airborne) and will return by courier if you prepay.

Publication

A few states require a new LLC to publish notice of formation in a newspaper. Usually, this must be in a *newspaper of general circulation*. In most cases, a small inexpensive newspaper, or *shopper*, can be used that will save hundreds of dollars over the rates of a big city daily newspaper. (Check the page for your state in Appendix A for the requirements.)

Membership or Management Agreement

As mentioned in the previous chapter, an LLC must decide if it will be managed by all the members or a limited number of managers. If it is to be run by managers, there may be one or more and he or she may be a member or not a member.

It is important, in either case, to have a written agreement spelling out the rights and duties of the members and managers, if any. This is also a good document in which to include other rules governing the LLC. Even if an LLC has only one member, a membership agreement should be signed to formalize the LLC and make it clear that the member is not personally liable for the debts of the business.

The law of LLCs is very new and since corporations that do not follow procedures can *have their veil pierced* (and their shareholders held liable), it is possible that a court may try the same with an LLC. So following the old formula is the safest. Of course, if you set up procedures and do not follow them, this could backfire and a court could use that as a reason to impose liability.

Membership Operating Agreement

Form 7 in Appendix C is a generic **Member-Managed Operating Agreement**. Use this form if your LLC will have one member or if it will have two or more members and be managed by all the members.

This form has basic terms that can be useful to most businesses. If all of the terms apply to your business, you should execute a copy and keep it with your company records.

If there are other terms you would like to include in your agreement, you can add them in paragraph 21 or draw up an *addendum* to the membership agreement.

Management Operating Agreement

Form 8 in Appendix C is a generic **MANAGEMENT OPERATING AGREEMENT**. Use this form if your LLC will have two or more members and be managed by a limited number of members or by someone who is not a member.

This form has basic terms which can be useful to most businesses. If all of the terms apply to your business, you should execute a copy and keep it with your company records.

If there are other terms you would like to include in your agreement, you can add them in paragraph 21 or draw up an addendum to the management agreement.

Schedule A

The operating agreements both use a "**SCHEDULE A**" to include the specific information for your company. (see form 9, p.235.)

Capitalization

Your new company will naturally need some money to get operations started. Some of this will be *capital* that you put into the business, but some may also be loans. Money that is set up as a loan can be later taken out tax-free. Therefore, it might seem good to start with all loans and little or no capital. But the danger is, if a business is *undercapitalized*, the owners may later be liable for some of its debts.

"What is enough capital for a business" is a legal question, and no one can say what a judge or jury may some day decide. If the business is a service company and needs little equipment other than ladders or computers, a couple thousand dollars would be fine. If the business needs a lot of expensive equipment, it would probably not be reasonable to put in $1,000 in capital and $99,000 in loans.

One way to know what is reasonable is to see what a bank would loan the company. If a company could put $5,000 down on its start-up equipment and borrow the rest, it would probably be reasonable to use $5,000 as capital and $95,000 as a loan from the owner.

If you are unsure if your intended capitalization is right, you could check a book on business accounting or with an accountant who works with start-up businesses.

If an existing business is being converted to an LLC, you may want to contribute the existing equipment as part, or all, of the start-up capital. To avoid potential liability, you should be sure not to value the equipment at more than the fair market value. To transfer the equipment to the company, you can use the **BILL OF SALE** in this book. (see form 6, p.229.)

In some instances, people wish to trade services for an interest in a business. For example, one person may contribute business equipment and the other work for three months without pay, for fifty-fifty ownership in the business. But in some states, this is not allowed. Check you state statute before setting up such an arrangement.

Tax Forms

In forming an LLC, there are two tax forms you will need to complete; **IRS FORM SS-4** and **IRS FORM 8832**.

Taxpayer Identification Number

Prior to opening a bank account, the limited liability company must obtain a *taxpayer identification number*—the business equivalent of a social security number. The fastest way to get the number is obtain it online. (If the IRS website is not running properly, you may need to follow up with a phone call to get the number.) Get the form at **www.irs.gov** by entering "SS-4" in the search box and clicking on "Online Application—Form SS-4."

You can also get the number by filing **IRS FORM SS-4**. (see form 3, p.209.) If you mail it in, it may take two or three weeks. If you fax it in, they will usually fax your number in a few days. If you need the number more quickly, you can obtain it by phone in twenty to forty minutes, depending on how long you are on hold. Be sure to have your completed **IRS FORM SS-4** in front of you when you call. The address, phone, and fax numbers are in the instructions with the form.

When you apply for this number, you will probably be put on the mailing list for other tax forms. If you do not receive these, you should call your local IRS forms number and request the forms for new businesses. These include Circular E explaining the taxes due, the W-4 forms for each employee, the tax deposit coupons, and the Form 941 quarterly return for withholding.

Form 8832

IRS FORM 8832 was issued by the IRS in 1997 to allow LLCs to chose their tax status. (see form 4, p.217.) It is essentially a choice between partnership taxation and corporate taxation. For a single-member LLC, it is a choice between sole proprietorship taxation and corporate taxation.

The difference in taxation is that a sole proprietorship or partnership is not taxed at all, but a corporation is treated like a separate taxpayer. A sole proprietorship or partnership reports its income and expenses and the proprietor or partners report the net profit or loss on their personal tax return. A corporation files a tax return and pays tax on any profits, and if it distributes any of the profits to the members, those profits are taxed again. Therefore, in most cases it is better to choose partnership taxation.

One way around the double taxation is if all of the profits can be paid to the members as salary, they are deductible and the corporation has no profit on which to pay tax. The problem arises when the company makes more money than would be reasonable to pay as salaries. The IRS can then impose extra corporate taxation on the excess amounts.

If you are unsure how you wish to be taxed, you should consult a book on taxation of businesses or check with a tax professional. Once you decide, you should complete **IRS FORM 8832**. If you elect to pass through taxation, you do not need to file the form—just give it to the members to file with their annual returns. If you elect corporate taxation, you need to file the form within seventy-five days.

Form 2553

If you elect to be taxed as a corporation, and if you would like that to be S corporation status rather than C corporation status, then you must file Form 2553 within seventy-five days of starting your business.

Employees

An LLC that has employees other than its members is subject to numerous laws and reporting requirements, which are beyond the scope of this book. These include new hire reporting, federal wage withholding, state and federal unemployment compensation taxes, discrimination laws, minimum wage laws, and numerous posters that must be placed in the workplace regarding child labor laws and health and safety issues.

Bank Accounts

A limited liability company must have a bank account. Checks payable to a limited liability company cannot be cashed—they must be deposited into an account.

Unfortunately, many banks charge companies for the right to put their money in the bank. For similar balance and activity between a personal account and a corporate account, an individual might earn $6.00 interest for the month while a corporation pays $40.00 in bank fees. The bank is not losing money on every personal account, so the corporate account is simply generating $46.00 more in profit for the bank.

Fortunately, some banks have set up reasonable fees for small businesses, such as charging no fees if a balance of $1000 or $2500 is maintained. Because the fees can easily amount to hundreds of dollars a year, it pays to shop around. Even if the bank is relatively far from the business, using bank-by-mail can make the distance meaningless. However, do not be surprised if a bank raises its initial low fees. A company could change banks four times in one year as each one raises its fees or is bought out by a bank with higher fees.

One method for avoiding high bank fees is to open a checking account and a *money market account*. (Money market accounts pay higher interest and usually do not charge for making deposits. You can only write three checks a month, but you can usually make unlimited withdrawals.) Make all of your deposits into the money market account and pay bills out of the regular checking account, transferring funds as needed. Some banks also charge for deposits into money market accounts, so start one at a brokerage firm.

Another way to save money is to order checks from a private source rather than through the bank. These are usually much cheaper than those the bank offers because the bank makes a profit on the check printing. If the bank officer does not like the idea when you are opening the account, just wait until your first batch runs out and switch over without telling the bank. They probably will not notice, as long as you get the checks printed correctly. Most *business checks* are large and expensive. There is no reason you cannot use small *personal size checks* for your business.

All you should need to open a company bank account is a copy of your Articles of Incorporation and your Federal Tax Identification Number. If you have trouble opening the account, you can use the **BANKING RESOLUTION** (see form 12, p.241) included with this book, or you can make up a similar form.

Licenses

Counties and municipalities in most states are authorized to levy a license tax on the right to do business. Before opening your business, you should obtain a county occupational license, and if you will be working within a city, a city occupational license. Businesses that work in several cities, such as builders, must obtain a license from each city in which they will work. This does not have to be done until you actually begin a job in a particular city.

County occupational licenses can usually be obtained from the tax collector in the county courthouse. City licenses are usually available at city hall. Be sure to find out if *zoning* allows your type of business before buying or leasing property because the licensing departments will check the zoning before issuing your license.

Problems occasionally arise when a person attempts to start a business in his or her home. Small new businesses cannot afford to pay rent for commercial space and cities often try to forbid business in residential areas. Getting a county occupational license often gives notice to the city that a business is being conducted in a residential area.

Some people avoid the problem by starting their businesses without occupational licenses, figuring that the penalties are nowhere near the cost of office space. Others get the county license and ignore the city rules. If a person has commercial trucks and equipment parked on his or her property, there will probably be complaints by neighbors, and the city will most likely take legal action. But if a person's business consists merely of making phone calls out of the home and keeping supplies inside the house, the problem may never arise.

If a problem does occur regarding a home business that does not disturb the neighbors, a good argument can be made that the zoning law is unconstitutional. When zoning laws were first instituted, they were not meant to stop people from doing things in a residence that had historically been part of the life in a residence. Consider a painter. Should a zoning law prohibit a person from sitting in his home and painting pictures? If he or she sells them for a living is there a difference? Can the government force him or her to rent commercial space?

Similar arguments can be made for many home businesses. But court battles with a city are expensive and probably not worth the effort for a small business. The best course of action is to keep a low profile. Using a post office box is sometimes helpful in diverting attention away from the residence. However, the secretary of state and the occupational license administrator will usually demand a street address. In most areas, there should be no problem using a residential address and explaining to the city that it is merely the corporate address and that no business is conducted on the premises. As always, check with your state's individual laws before committing to anything.

Checklist for Forming an LLC

❏ Decide on a company name

❏ Search the name to be sure it is not already taken

❏ Prepare and file ARTICLES OF ORGANIZATION and any other organizational form required by the state

❏ Decide on capitalization and tax status

❏ Obtain Federal Employer Identification Number **(IRS FORM SS-4)**

❏ Prepare **IRS FORM 8832** and file it within seventy-five days if you are choosing corporate taxation

❏ Prepare and file **FORM 2553** if S corporation status desired (file within seventy-five days of start-up)

❏ Prepare MEMBERSHIP OPERATING AGREEMENT or MANAGEMENT OPERATING AGREEMENT

❏ If necessary, meet with securities lawyer regarding nonparticipating members

❏ Hold organizational meeting

    ❏ Complete OPERATING AGREEMENT

    ❏ Complete BILL OF SALE if property is traded for interest

❏ File fictitious or assumed name registration if one will be used

❏ Get city or county licenses, if needed

❏ Open bank account

Chapter 6:
Membership Interests
in an LLC

Before setting up your LLC, you need to determine its financial structure as well as a plan for future expansion.

Capital Structure

There is no hard-and-fast rule as to how much capital you should put into a limited liability company. The more you assign as capital, the more you have at risk in the business. Therefore, you want to deposit as little as possible. Keep in mind that if you contribute too little, a court might some day say you were undercapitalized and find you personally liable for company debts, just as it could for a corporation. Also, there could be tax problems with not counting enough of your contributions as capital or for contributing appreciated property. These matters should be discussed with a tax specialist.

If you are starting a small business that does not need a lot of expensive equipment, a few thousand dollars would be a safe amount with which to start. If you need to buy expensive equipment, and the company can borrow the money from a third party to cover it, you would probably be safe as well. However, if you need to purchase expensive equipment and personally loan the money to the company rather than contribute it as capital, you should weigh the risks of a lawsuit and consider consulting an attorney or accountant who specializes in business start-ups.

One thing to keep in mind is that if you do not put in the amount of capital stated in your initial agreement and are later sued or file bankruptcy, you may be required to come up with any unpaid amount because it may be considered an unpaid debt to the company. That is something for which you could be held personally liable. In a grievous case, a judge might use it as a reason to void the limited liability of the LLC.

Payment for Membership Interests

Most states allow membership interests to be paid with money, property, services, or a promissory note. The important thing to remember is if a member fails to make the specified payment or takes the money back out (other than salary or profit), he or she may be liable to the company or its creditors for the full amount that should have been paid.

Some other things to consider include the following.

- If a member trades services for an interest in the capital of the company, he or she must pay income tax on the value of interest at the time the services are exchanged for the interest. (If the interest is only a share of future profits, the tax does not have to be paid until the profits are received.)
- When appreciated property is traded to an LLC in exchange for a membership interest, the tax basis of the property carries over to the membership interest. Taxes on the appreciation are paid when the member sells his or her LLC interest.
- If the LLC sells the property, it may have to pay a tax on the amount received over the contributor's basis.

Tax rules are complicated and ever-changing. If you will be doing creative financing, you should consult with a tax expert or a tax guide.

Securities Laws

The issuance of *securities* is subject to both federal and state securities laws. A *security* can either be an equity interest in a company (stock, membership) or debt (notes, bonds, etc.). The laws covering securities are so broad that any instrument representing an investment in an enterprise where the investor is relying on the efforts of others for profit is considered a security. Even a *promissory note* has been held to be a security. Once an investment is determined to involve a security, strict rules apply. If the rules are not followed, there can be criminal penalties and civil damages can be awarded to purchasers.

The rules are designed to protect people who put up money as an investment in a business. In the stock market crash of the 1930s, many people lost their life savings in swindles, and the government wants to be sure that it will not happen again. Unfortunately, the laws can also make it difficult to raise capital for many honest businesses.

The goal of the laws covering sales of securities is that investors be given full disclosure of the risks involved in an investment. To accomplish this, the law usually requires that the securities must either be registered with the *Federal Securities and Exchange Commission* or a similar state regulatory body, and that lengthy disclosure statements be compiled and distributed.

The law is complicated and strict compliance is required. The penalties are so harsh that most lawyers will not handle securities matters. You most likely would not be able to get through the registration process on your own. But, like your decision to form your LLC without a lawyer, you may wish to consider some alternatives when attempting to raise capital without a lawyer.

◆ Borrow the money as a personal loan from friends or relatives. The disadvantage is that you will have to pay them back personally if the business fails. However, you may have to do that anyway if they are close relatives or if you do not follow the securities laws.

◆ Tailor your stock issuance to fall within the exemptions in the securities laws. There are some exemptions in the securities laws for small businesses that may apply to your transaction. (The anti-fraud provisions always apply even if the transaction is exempt from registration.) Some exemptions are explained below, but you should make at least one appointment with a securities lawyer to be sure you have covered everything and that there have not been any changes in the law. Often, you can pay for an hour or so of a securities lawyer's time for $100 or $200 and ask questions about your plans. He or she can tell you what not to do and what your options are. You can then make an informed decision.

Federal Exemptions from Securities Laws

In most situations where one person, a husband and wife, or a few partners run a business, and all parties are active in the enterprise, securities laws do not apply to their issuance of membership interests to themselves. As a practical matter, if a relative of yours wants to put up some money for some stock in your business, you might not get in trouble. They probably will not seek triple damages and criminal penalties if your business fails.

However, you may wish to obtain money from additional investors to enable your business to grow. This can be done in many circumstances as long as you follow the rules carefully. In some cases, you do not have to file anything with the Securities and Exchange Commission (SEC) but in others, you must file a notice.

Federal Private Placement Exemption

If you sell interests in your business to a small group of people without any advertising, you can fall into the private offering exemption if the following are true:

◆ all persons to whom offers are made are financially astute, are participants in the business, or have a substantial net worth;

◆ no advertising or general solicitation is used to promote the stock;

◆ the number of persons to whom the offers are made is limited;

◆ the shares are purchased for investment and not for immediate resale;

- ◆ the persons to whom the interest is offered are given all relevant information (including financial information) regarding the issuance and the corporation. Again, there are numerous court cases explaining each aspect of these rules, including such questions as what defines a *financially astute* person; and,
- ◆ a filing claiming the exemption is made upon the United States Securities and Exchange Commission.

Federal Intrastate Offering Exemption

If you only offer your securities to residents of one state, you may be exempt from federal securities laws. This is because federal laws usually only apply to interstate commerce. Intrastate offerings are covered by SEC Rule 147, and if it is followed carefully, your sale will be exempt from federal registration.

Federal Small Offerings Exemptions

In recent years the SEC has liberalized the rules in order to make it easier for business to grow. Under Regulation D adopted by the Securities and Exchange Commission, there are three types of exemptions under rules 504, 505, and 506.

- ◆ Under SEC Rule 504, the offering of securities of up to $1,000,000 in a twelve month period can be exempt. Offers can be made to any number of persons, no specific information must be provided, and investors do not have to be sophisticated.
- ◆ Under SEC Rule 505, offering of up to $5,000,000 can be made in a twelve month period but no public advertising may be used, and only thirty-five non-accredited investors may purchase stock. Any number of *accredited investors* may purchase stock. (Accredited investors are sophisticated individuals with high net worth or high income, large trusts or investment companies, or persons involved in the business.)
- ◆ Under SEC Rule 506, there is no limit on the amount of money that may be raised, but like Rule 505, it does not allow advertising and limits non-accredited investors to thirty-five.

State Securities Laws

One reason there are exemptions from federal securities laws is there are so many state laws covering securities, that additional registration is not needed. Every state has securities laws, called *blue sky laws*. If you wish to offer your stock in all fifty states, you must be registered in all fifty states unless you can fit into one of the exemptions. However, exemptions are very limited.

Typical State Law Private Placement Exemption

The most common one is the private placement exemption. This can apply if all of the following are true:

- there are thirty-five or fewer purchasers of shares;
- no commissions are paid to anyone to promote the stock;
- no advertising or general solicitation is used to promote the stock;
- all material information (including financial information) regarding the stock issuance and the company is given or is accessible to all shareholders; and,
- a three day right of recision is given.

These rules may sound simple, but there are many more rules, regulations, and court cases explaining each one in more detail. For example, what does "thirty-five persons" mean? Sounds simple, but it can mean more than thirty-five persons. Spouses, persons whose *net worth* exceeds a million dollars, and founders of the company may not be counted in some circumstances.

As you can see, the exemption does not give you much latitude in raising money. Therefore, if you wish to raise money from a wider group of people, you will have to register. To find out more about your state's requirements, contact the securities commission of your state. The address is in the back of this chapter.

Blue Sky Reporter

Another good source of information concerning the securities laws of all fifty states is the *Blue Sky Reporter*, a multi-volume loose leaf service that summarizes the securities laws of the states. A copy should be available in most law libraries.

State Laws

You can link to the securities laws of each state through the website of the North American Securities Administrators Association, Inc., located at **www.nasaa.org**.

Internet Stock Sales

With the advent of the Internet, promoters of business interests have a new way of reaching large numbers of people. However, all securities laws apply to the Internet, and they are being enforced. Recently, state attorney generals have issued cease and desist orders to promoters not registered in their states.

Under current law, you must be registered in a state in order to sell stock to its residents. You must turn down any residents who want to buy your stock if you are not registered in that state.

You may wonder how the famous Spring Street Brewing raised $1.6 million for its Wit Beer on the Internet. The main reason they were successful was because their president is a securities lawyer and could prepare his own prospectus to file with the SEC and the states. That would have cost anyone else about $100,000. Also, most of their stock sales were inspired by newspaper and magazine articles about them and not from the Internet.

The lawyer who marketed Wit Beer's shares on the Internet has started a business to advise others on raising capital. It is located at the following address.

Wit Capital
826 Broadway
New York, NY 10003

Some Internet sites that may be helpful in raising capital are:

America's Business Funding Directory: www.businessfinance.com
Angel Capital Electronic Network (SBA): www.sba.gov
FinanceHub: www.financehub.com
NVST: www.nvst.com

Payment for Membership Interests

When issuing stock, it is important that full payment be made by the purchasers. If the shares have a par value, and the payment is cash, the cash must not be less than the par value. In most states, promissory notes cannot be used in payment for shares. The shares must not be issued until the payment has been received by the corporation.

Trading Property for Interests

In many cases, organizers of a corporation have property they want to contribute for use in starting up the business. This is often the case when an on-going business is incorporated. To avoid future problems, the property should be traded at a fair value for the shares, and the directors should pass a resolution stating that they agree with the value of the property. When the stock certificate is issued in exchange for the property, a bill of sale should be executed by the owner of the property detailing everything which is being exchanged for the stock.

Taxable Transactions

In cases where property is exchanged for something of value, such as stock, there is often income tax due as if there had been a sale of the property. Fortunately, Section 351 of the IRS Code allows tax-free exchange of property for stock, if the persons receiving the stock for the property or for cash *end up owning* at least eighty percent of the voting and other stock in the corporation. If more than twenty percent of the stock is issued in exchange for services instead of property or cash, the transfers of property will be taxable and treated as a sale for cash.

Trading Services for Interests

In some cases, the founders of an LLC wish to issue membership interests to one or more persons in exchange for their services to the business. It has always been possible to issue interests for services which have previously been performed. Some states make it unlawful to issue interests for promises to perform services in the future. Check your state's LLC statute if you plan to do this.

State Securities Registration Offices

The following are the addresses of the state offices that handle registration of securities. You can contact them for information on their requirements.

Alabama Securities Commission
770 Washington Street
Suite 570
Montgomery, AL 36130-4700
Phone: 334-242-2984 or 800-222-1253
Fax: 334-242-0240 or 334-353-4690
www.asc.state.al.us

**Alaska Department of Commerce
and Economic Development
Division of Banking, Securities, and Corporations**
P.O. Box 110807
Juneau, AK 99811-0807
Phone: 907-465-2521
Fax: 907-465-2549
www.dced.state.ak.us/bsc

**Arizona Corporation Commission
Securities Division**
1300 West Washington Street
3rd Floor
Phoenix, AZ 85007
Phone: 602-542-4242
Fax: 602-594-7470
www.ccsd.cc.state.az.us

Arkansas Securities Department
Heritage West Building
201 East Markham
3rd Floor
Little Rock, AR 72201
Phone: 501-324-9260
Fax: 501-324-9268

**California Department of Corporations
Securities Regulation Division**
320 West 4th Street
Suite 750
Los Angeles, CA 90013-2344
Phone: 213-576-7500
Fax: 213-576-7179
www.corp.ca.gov/srd/security.htm

Colorado Division of Securities
1580 Lincoln Street
Suite 420
Denver, CO 80203
Phone: 303-894-2320
Fax: 303-861-2126
www.dora.state.co.us/securities

Connecticut Securities Division
260 Constitution Plaza
Hartford, CT 06103-1800
Phone: 860-240-8230
Fax: 860-240-8295
www.state.ct.us/dob

Delaware Department of Justice
Division of Securities
820 North French Street, 5th Floor
Wilmington, DE 19801
Phone: 302-577-8242
Fax: 302-577-6987
www.state.de.us/securities/index.htm

District of Columbia
Department of Insurance and Securities Regulation
810 First Street
Suite 701
Washington, DC 20002
Phone: 202-727-8000
Fax: 202-535-1196
http://disb.dc.gov/disr/site/default.asp

Florida Division of Securities and Finance
200 East Gaines Street
Tallahassee, FL 32399-0300
Phone: 850-410-9805
Fax: 850-410-9748
www.dbf.state.fl.us/licensing

Georgia Secretary of State
Securities and Business
Regulation Division
2 Martin Luther King Jr. Drive, S.E.
Suite 802, West Tower
Atlanta, GA 30334
Phone: 404-656-3920
Fax: 404-657-8410
www.sos.state.ga.us/securities
or www.georgiasecurities.org

Hawaii Department of Commerce
and Consumer Affairs
Commissioner of Securities
P. O. Box 40
Honolulu, HI 96810
Phone: 808-586-2744
Fax: 808-586-3977
www.hawaii.gov/dcca/areas/sec/

Idaho Department of Finance
700 West State Street
2nd Floor
P.O. Box 83702
Boise, ID 83720-0031
Phone: 208-332-8000
Fax: 208-332-8099
http://finance.state.id.us

Illinois Securities Department
Jefferson Terrace
Suite 300 A
300 West Jefferson Street
Springfield, IL 62702
Phone: 217-782-2256
Fax: 217-782-8876
www.sos.state.il.us/departments/securities/home.html

Indiana Securities Division
302 West Washington Street
Room E-111
Indianapolis, IN 46204
Phone: 317-232-6681 or 800-223-8791
Fax: 317-233-3675
www.IN.gov/sos/securities

Iowa Securities Bureau
340 Maple Street
Des Moines, IA 50319-0066
Phone: 515-281-4441
Fax: 515-281-3059
www.iowa.gov

Kansas Securities Commissioner
Office of the Securities Commissioner
618 South Kansas Avenue
Topeka, KS 66603-3804
Phone: 785-296-3307
Fax: 785-296-6872
www.securities.state.ks.us

Kentucky Department of Financial Institutions
1025 Capital Center Drive
Suite 200
Frankfort, KY 40601
Phone: 502-573-3390 or 800-223-2579
Fax: 502-573-8787
www.dfi.state.ky.us

Louisiana Office of Financial Institutions
Securities Division
Commissioner of Securitites
8660 United Plaza Boulevard
2nd Floor
Baton Rouge, LA 70809
Phone: 225-925-4660
Fax: 225-925-4548
www.ofi.state.la.us

Maine Department of Professional and
Financial Regulation
Office of Securities
121 State House Station
Augusta, ME 04333
Phone: 207-624-8551
Fax: 207-624-8590
www.state.me.us/pfr/sec/sec_index.htm

Maryland Securities Division
200 Saint Paul Place
Baltimore, MD 21202
Phone: 410-576-6360
www.oag.state.md.us/securities/index.htm

Massachusetts Securities Division
One Ashburton Place
17th Floor
Boston, MA 02108
Phone: 617-727-3548 or 800-269-5428
Fax: 617-248-0177
www.state.ma.us/sec/sct/sctidx.htm

Michigan Department of
Consumer and Industry Services
Offices of Financial and Insurance Services
P.O. Box 30220
Lansing, MI 48909
Phone: 517-373-0220 or 877-999-6442
Fax: 517-335-4978
www.michigan.gov/cis

Minnesota Department of Commerce
85 7th Place East
Suite 500
St. Paul, MN 55101
Phone: 651-296-4973
www.state.mn.us

Mississippi Securities Division
P.O. Box 136
Jackson, MS 39205
Phone: 800-804-6364
Fax: 601-359-2663
www.sos.state.ms.us

Office of the Missouri Secretary of State
Securities Division
600 West Main Street
2nd Floor
Jefferson City, MO 65101
Phone: 573-751-4136
Fax: 573-526-3124
www.sos.mo.gov/securities

Montana Office of the State Auditor
Securities Division
840 Helena Avenue
Helena, MT 59601
Phone: 406-444-3246
Fax: 406-444-3497
www.discoveringmontana.com/sao/securities

Nebraska Bureau of Securities
Commerce Court
1230 "O" Street
Suite 400
P.O. Box 95006
Lincoln, NE 68509-5006
Phone: 402-471-3445
www.ndbf.org

Nevada Securities Division
555 East Washington Avenue
Suite 5200
Las Vegas, NV 89101
Phone: 702-486-2440
Fax: 702-486-2452
www.sos.state.nv.us/securities/index.htm

New Hampshire Bureau of Securities Regulation
State House
Room 204
Concord, NH 03301-4989
Phone: 603-271-1463
Fax: 603-271-7933
webster.state.nh.us/sos/securities

New Jersey Bureau of Securities
P.O. Box 47029
Newark, NJ 07101
Phone: 973-504-3600
Fax: 973-504-3601
www.state.nj.us/lps/ca/bos.htm

New Mexico Securities Division
Regulation and Licensing Department
2550 Cerrillos Road
3rd Floor
Santa Fe, NM 87505
Phone: 505-827-7010
Fax: 505-827-7095
www.rld.state.nm.us/sec/index.htm

New York State
Attorney General's Office
Investors and Securities
The Capital
Albany, NY 12224-0341
Phone: 212-416-8000
Fax: 212-416-8816
www.oag.state.ny.us/investors/investors.html

North Carolina Securities Division
Department of the Secretary of State
P.O. Box 29622
Raleigh, NC 27626-0622
Phone: 919-733-3924
Fax: 919-733-5172
www.secretary.state.nc.us/sec

North Dakota Securities Commission
State Capitol
5th Floor
600 East Boulevard Avenue
Bismarck, ND 58505-0510
Phone: 701-328-2910
Fax: 701-328-2946
www.ndsecurities.com

Ohio Department of Commerce
Division of Securities
77 South High Street
22nd Floor
Columbus, OH 43215
Phone: 614-644-7381
www.securities.state.oh.us

Oklahoma Department of Securities
Suite 860, First National Center
120 North Robinson
Oklahoma City, OK 73102
Phone: 405-280-7700
Fax: 405-280-7742
www.securities.state.ok.us

**Oregon Department of Consumer
and Business Services
Division of Finance and Corporate Securities**
P.O. Box 14480
Salem, OR 97309-0405
Phone: 503-378-4140
Fax: 503-947-7862
www.cbs.state.or.us/external/dfcs

**Pennsylvania Division of Corporation Finance
Pennsylvania Securities Commission**
Eastgate Office Building
2nd Floor
1010 North 7th Street
Harrisburg, PA 17102-1410
Phone: 717-787-8061
Fax: 717-783-5122
www.psc.state.pa.us

Puerto Rico Commissioner of Financial Institutions
Centro Europa Building
1492 Ponce de Leon Avenue
Suite 600
San Juan, PR 00907-4127
Phone: 787-723-3131
Fax: 787-723-4255
www.cif.gov.pr/valores_eng.html

South Carolina Securities Division
P.O. Box 11549
Columbia, SC 29211-1549
Phone: 803-734-9916
Fax: 803-734-3677
www.scsecurities.org/index.html

South Dakota Division of Securities
445 East Capitol Avenue
Pierre, SD 57501
Phone: 605-773-4823
Fax: 605-773-5953
www.state.sd.us/dcr/securities/security.htm

**Tennessee Department of Commerce and Insurance
Securities Division**
500 James Robertson Parkway
Suite 680
Davy Crockett Tower
Nashville, TN 37243-0583
Phone: 615-741-3187
Fax: 615-532-8375
www.state.tn.us/commerce

Texas State Securities Board
P.O. Box 13167
Austin, Texas 78711-3167
Phone: 512-305-8300
Fax: 512-305-8310
www.ssb.state.tx.us

**Utah Department of Commerce
Division of Securities**
Box 146760
Salt Lake City, Utah 84114-6760
Phone: 801-530-6600
Fax: 801-530-6980
www.securities.state.ut.us

**Vermont Securities Division
Department of Banking, Insurance, Securities and
Health Care Administration**
89 Main Street
Drawer 20
Montpelier, VT 05620-3101
Phone: 802-828-3420
www.bishca.state.vt.us/securitiesdiv/securindex.htm

Virginia State Corporation Commission
P.O. Box 1197
Richmond, VA 23218
Phone: 804-371-9967
Fax: 804-371-9911
www.scc.virginia.gov

Washington Department of Financial Institutions
Securities Division
P.O. Box 9033
Olympia, Washington 98507-9033
Phone: 360-902-8760
Fax: 360-902-0524
www.dfi.wa.gov

West Virginia Securities Division
State Capitol Building 1
Room W-100
Charleston, WV 25305
Phone: 304-558-2257
Fax: 304-558-4211
www.wvauditor.com

Wisconsin Division of Securities
P.O. Box 8041
Madison, WI 53708-8041
Phone: 608-264-7969
Fax: 608-264-7968
www.wdfi.org/fi/securities

Wyoming Securities Division
Secretary of the State
The Capital Building
Room 109
200 West 24th Street
Cheyenne, WY 82002-0020
Phone: 307-777-7370
Fax: 307-777-5339
http://soswy.state.wy.us/securiti/securiti.htm

Chapter 7:
Running a Limited Liability Company

One benefit of the limited liability company is the lack of requirements needed to comply with the formalities of a corporation. It is not yet totally clear what, if any, requirements courts may impose. Though it is widely recognized that the requirements will be less strict than for a corporation, to be safe, it is best to have some formalities such as keeping minutes and records.

Day-to-Day Activities

As previously mentioned, every LLC should have an operating agreement. This usually contains some formalities for the operation of the company. The important thing is that, if there are formalities in the document, you should follow them.

Minutes

In most states, the keeping of *minutes* is not specifically required of an LLC, but it is a simple act which may be helpful in proving that the LLC followed enough formalities to be legitimate. Whenever the company takes some major action, such as leasing a new office or granting bonuses, you should prepare minutes reflecting the decision. A blank **MINUTES** form that does not take much time to fill out is included in this book. (see form 10, p.237.) Keep several blank copies with your company papers so you will have them on hand when you need them.

One important point to remember is to keep the company separate from your personal affairs. Do not continuously make loans to yourself from company funds, and do not commingle funds.

Another important point to remember is always use the name of the company with the correct suffix (LLC, LC, etc.). Always sign company documents as a member of the company acting for the company, like this:

Happy Daze, LLC

By _____*Joe Daze*_____ Member

If you do not, you may lose your protection from liability. There have been cases where a person forgot to put his title after his name and was held personally liable for a company debt.

Member Meetings

There is no requirement for regular meetings of the members. But, once again, since the law is not settled in this area, the more formality you use, the greater protection you have.

Holding a meeting when major decisions are being made is a good idea. If you are a one-member company you can hold the meeting in your head. Just remember to fill out a minutes form and put it with the company records.

Records

Each state has its own statute controlling whether or not records need to be kept, and if so, what types. A summary for each state is included in Appendix A. However, since the laws may change you should get a copy of the section of your state's law to be sure you are in compliance. Typically the following types of things need to be kept on file:

◆ a current list of the names and last known addresses of all members;

◆ a copy of the Articles of Organization, plus any amendments;

◆ copies of the company's income tax returns for the last three years;

◆ copies of any regulations or member agreements currently in effect;

◆ copies of any financial statements for the company for the last three years; and,

◆ the amount of cash and the agreed value of any property or services contributed by each member or agreed to be contributed by each member.

Annual Reports

In most states, an LLC must file a report each year (or in some states every two years). This is to let the state keep an up-to-date record of the status of the company, and in many states the fee is small. But in some states, the annual report is a way to raise revenue, and the fee is hundreds of dollars.

In most states, the report is a preprinted form with the company name, address, and member names, which needs to be signed and returned.

Failure to file your annual report on time can result in your company being dissolved. In some states the fee for reinstatement is over $500, so do not miss the deadline!

Chapter 8:
Amending
a Limited Liability Company

It is usually advisable to draft your LLC documents in broad language so that they cover most situations which may arise. However, when there are major changes in the LLC, you may have to amend some of your documents.

Articles of Organization

Since the **ARTICLES OF ORGANIZATION** are on file with the secretary of state or other filing office, any amendments to them will have to be filed and a filing fee paid. In some states, the fee is quite high, so if you can accomplish your changes without amending the Articles, it would save time and money.

Required Amendments

To prepare an amendment, you should first check your state's statute to be sure that you include all information required and to see if it must be notarized or comply with any other requirements.

There are certain types of changes, such as a change of the company name or registered agent, for which you are required to file an amendment. In general, these are any things contained in the original **ARTICLES OF ORGANIZATION**.

Restated Articles

Some states allow you to file *restated articles*. This is done when a company has had several amendments to its articles and wishes to write a fresh copy deleting obsolete clauses and incorporating new clauses.

Raising Capital Contributions

In some states, you are required to amend the articles if you change the capital contributions. This may require a substantial filing fee. A cheaper alternative would be to make a loan to the company rather than increase capital. Check with your accountant, or review a good tax guide to be sure the company is not undercapitalized.

Membership or Management Agreement

Your *membership agreement* or *management agreement* should contain a section explaining the procedure for making amendments. Be sure to follow this procedure when making amendments. Otherwise, a court could use your failure as a reason to impose liability on the members.

Registered Agent or Registered Office

If your registered agent or registered office changes, you must file this information as soon as it is effective and pay a filing fee. Many states have a form on which to do this. In case you neglect to do so, in most states, you can include the change on your annual report. By waiting until your annual report is due to make the change, you may be able to avoid an extra filing fee. (But in some states you have to pay extra to change the agent.)

Merging with Another Business

Merging with another business is usually somewhat complicated from both a tax and legal standpoint. Many states have extensive merger requirements in their LLC statutes. Before executing your plan, be sure to learn the tax implications and to check the statutes for the requirements.

Chapter 9:
Dissolving a Limited Liability Company

At some point you may decide to dissolve your LLC. This chapter explains the ways it can be done.

Automatic Dissolution

If your limited liability company has ceased to do business and you no longer need to keep it active, it is not necessary in most states to take any special action to dissolve it. It will automatically dissolve if you fail to file your annual report. If you decide to let your company dissolve this way, be sure that you will not need the company again—the fees for reinstatement can be high. You may need to pay annual fees for all previous years plus a penalty. The penalty can amount to several hundred dollars.

If your company has some debts that it is unable to pay at the time of dissolution, you would be better off to formally dissolve it or having it file bankruptcy. Otherwise, there is a chance you could be held personally liable for the debts.

Events Requiring Dissolution

In some states, there are specific events which require an LLC to dissolve. Two examples are if a set term has expired, or if a member dies and there is no provision for continuation after death. In the few remaining states still requiring two members, the withdrawal of one would require dissolution as well. In cases like these, the remaining members are usually required to file a form which formally dissolves the company.

Articles of Dissolution

An advantage of formal dissolution is that, in most cases, if you give proper notice to creditors, after a period of time, there is no risk that they can come back against the members.

To formally dissolve a limited liability company, *Articles of Dissolution* are usually filed with the secretary of state. The procedure varies somewhat by state so check your state's statute for specific requirements.

After dissolution, an LLC may not carry on business, but in many states it can continue its existence for the purpose of:

- ◆ collecting its assets;
- ◆ disposing of property which will not be distributed to members;
- ◆ discharging liabilities;
- ◆ distributing assets to creditors and members; and,
- ◆ doing anything else necessary to wind up its affairs.

Revocation of Dissolution

In some states, an LLC may "undissolve" within a certain length of time after filing Articles of Dissolution by filing *Articles of Revocation of Dissolution.* Check your state statute if you need to do this.

Judicial Dissolution

A court may dissolve an LLC under certain circumstances. This can usually be initiated by a legal department of the state, a creditor, a member, or the LCC itself. State law controls this type of action, but there is also a chance that one of the parties can bring the business into bankruptcy court which is controlled by federal bankruptcy laws.

Distribution of Assets

When an LLC dissolves, its assets must be distributed as required by state law. In most cases, this will include:

- ◆ creditors, including members who are creditors;
- ◆ members and creators in satisfaction of liabilities; and,
- ◆ members in proportion to their capital accounts.

See your state's statute for more information.

Bankruptcy

If your company is in debt beyond its means, it can file for bankruptcy. *Chapter 7* bankruptcy is for liquidation in which all of the assets of the company are sold and divided among the preferred creditors. *Chapter 11* is for reorganization of debts where the company hopes that by extending the payment terms of its obligations, it can eventually pay them and continue its business.

If an LLC files bankruptcy, this does not have to affect the credit of the members unless they have guaranteed some of the debts. In this case, they would have to either take over the debts or file bankruptcy themselves.

If the debts are small and there is little chance the creditors will pursue collection, bankruptcy is unnecessary. In this case, you can allow the state to dissolve the corporation for failure to file the annual report. However, if the debts are large and you fear the creditors will attempt to collect the debt from the members, you should go through formal bankruptcy and dissolution. Such a scenario is beyond the scope of this book, and you should consult an attorney or bankruptcy manual for further guidance.

For Further Reference

As mentioned earlier in this book, the LLC laws are new and still developing. To keep up-to-date on changes in the law, the following sites are good places to do legal research:

www.lawschool.cornell.edu/lawlibrary
www.findlaw.com

The following books provide in-depth analysis of LLC law. Some are expensive, but may be found in larger law libraries.

Callison, J. William, and Maureen A. Sullivan. *Limited Liability Companies: A State-by-State Guide to Law and Practice.* Eagan: West Group.

Cunningham, John M. *Drafting Limited Liability Company Operating Agreements.* New York: Aspen Publishers.

Rubenstein, Jeffrey C., et al. *Limited Liability Companies: Law, Practice and Forms.* Seattle: Shepards.

Tuthill, Walter C. *Limited Liability Companies: Legal Aspects of Organization, Operation, and Dissolution.* Washington, D.C.: BNA.

Glossary

The following definitions explain how the words are used in this book. (They may have other meanings in other contexts.)

A

accredited investor. Sophisticated individuals with high net worth or high income, large trusts or investment companies, or persons involved in the business.

addendum. A document attached to another document to add some new terms.

articles of organization. The legal document used to form a limited liability company that sets out basic information about it, such as its name.

assignment. The transfer of legal rights to another person or entity.

B

blue sky laws. Laws governing the sales of securities.

C

C corporation. A corporation that pays taxes on its profits.

capital. Initial funding of the business.

charging order. A court order directed at an interest in an LLC.

corporation. An artificial legal person that is set up to conduct a business owned by shareholders and run by officers and directors.

D

dissolution. The closing of a limited liability company.

distributions. Money paid out to owners of a corporation or limited liability company.

E

employee. Person who works for another under that person's control and direction.

employer identification number. Number issued by the Internal Revenue Service to identify taxpayers who do not have Social Security numbers.

F

fictitious name. A name used by a business that is not its personal or legal name.

G

general partnership. A business that is owned by two or more persons.

I

independent contractor. A person who does work as a separate business rather than as an employee.

industry code. A number assigned to each type of business.

insolvent. Being without enough assets of income to pay debts.

L

legal person. An entity recognized by the state as a person apart from its members.

liability. The legal responsibility to pay for an injury.

licensing board. A government entity which grants permission to perform certain functions.

limited liability. Fixing the amount a person can be forced to pay for a legal event at a limited sum.

limited liability company. An artificial legal person set up to conduct a business owned and run by members.

limited liability partnership. An artificial legal person set up to conduct a business owned and run by members, which is set up for professionals such as attorneys or doctors.

limited partnership. A business that is owned by two or more persons of which one or more is liable for the debts of the business and one or more has no liability for the debts.

M

management agreement. The document that controls the operation of a limited liability company that is managed by managers.

manager. A person who controls the operations of a limited liability company.

manager-managed LLC. A limited liability company that is controlled by one or more managers who are not all of the members of the company.

member. Person owning an interest in a limited liability company.

member-managed LLC. A limited liability company that is controlled by all of its members.

minority interest owners. The owners of an interest in an LLC who own less than a majority interest.

minutes. Records of the proceedings of business meetings.

N

natural person. A human being as opposed to a legal person created by the law.

net worth. The value of a person or an entity after subtracting liabilities from assets.

O

occupational license. A government-issued permit to transact business.

operating agreement. A contract among members of a limited liability company spelling out how the company is to be run.

organizational meeting. The meeting of the founders of a corporation or limited liability company in which company is structured and ready to begin business.

P

partnership. A business formed by two or more persons.

personal liability. Being forced to pay for a liability out of personal funds rather than from limited company assets.

piercing the corporate veil. When a court ignores the corporate structure to hold the owners of the business liable.

promissory note. A legal document in which a person promises to pay a sum of money.

promoters. Persons who start a business venture and usually offer interests for sale to investors.

proprietorship. A business that is owned by one person.

provisions. Terms of a legal document.

R

registered agent. A person who is designated by a limited liability company to receive legal papers for the company.

registered office. A physical location where the registered agent of a limited liability company can receive legal papers for the company.

regulations. The former name of the operating agreement of a limited liability company.

S

S corporation. A corporation in which the profits are taxed to the shareholders.

securities. Interests in a business such as stock or bonds.

T

tax basis. The amount used as the cost of an item for tax purposes.

trademark. A name or symbol used to identify the source of goods or services.

U

undercapitalized. Not having enough money to soundly operate.

unemployment compensation. Payments to a former employee who was terminated from a job for a reason not based on his or her fault.

uniform business report. A form filed annually by an LLC in some states.

Z

zoning. Laws that regulate the use of real estate.

Appendix A:
State-by-State LLC Statutes

The following pages contain a listing of each state's limited liability company laws and fees. Because the laws are constantly being changed by state legislatures, you should call before filing your papers to confirm the fees and other requirements. The phone numbers are provided for each state.

With the continued growth of the Internet, more and more state corporation divisions are making their forms, fees, and requirements available online. Some states have downloadable forms available, and some even allow you to search their entire database from the comfort of your home or office.

The current websites at the time of publication of this book are included for each state. However, the sites change constantly, so you may need to look a little deeper if your state's site has changed its address.

Note: *Not all states have a sample form.*

Alabama

Secretary of State
Corporations Division
P.O. Box 5616
Montgomery, AL 36103-5616
334-242-5324

Website:
www.sos.state.al.us/business/corporations.cfm

WHAT THEY SUPPLY:

State provides fill-in-the-blank Articles of Organization with short instructions and a help sheet.

WHAT MUST BE FILED:

You must file the original and two copies of the Articles of Organization in the county where the LLC's registered office is located. The probate court judge will receive and record the original Articles. Within thirty days of filing, a completed report (provided by the secretary of state with the filing package) must be filed with the Judge of Probate ($5 filing fee).

NAME REQUIREMENTS:

The name must contain the words "Limited Liability Company" or "L.L.C."

A name reservation for an LLC is not possible.

ARTICLES SPECIAL REQUIREMENTS:

The Articles must set forth the rights, terms, and conditions to admit additional members, and, if given, the right by remaining members to continue business after dissociation.

FILING FEES:

There is a filing fee of $40, payable to the "secretary of state" plus an additional $35 filing fee for the probate court judge (separate check).

REPORTS:

As stated above, the first report must be filed within thirty days after filing the Articles of Organization with a $5 fee with the Judge of Probate.

RECORDS REQUIRED:

- Names and addresses of members and managers
- Articles and all amendments
- Three years of financial records
- Three years of tax returns
- Operating agreement and all amendments

STATUTES:

Code of Alabama, Title 10, Chapter 12, Alabama Limited Liability Company Act.

STATE OF ALABAMA

DOMESTIC LIMITED LIABILITY COMPANY
ARTICLES OF ORGANIZATION GUIDELINES

INSTRUCTIONS:
STEP 1: THE NAME OF THE LIMITED LIABILITY COMPANY MUST CONTAIN THE WORDS LIMITED LIABILITY COMPANY, LLC OR L.L.C.
STEP 2: FILE THE ORIGINAL AND TWO COPIES OF THE ARTICLES OF ORGANIZATION IN THE COUNTY WHERE THE LLC'S REGISTERED OFFICE IS LOCATED. THE SECRETARY OF STATE'S FILING FEE IS $40. PLEASE CONTACT THE JUDGE OF PROBATE TO VERIFY THE PROBATE FILING FEE.

PURSUANT TO THE ALABAMA LIMITED LIABILITY COMPANY ACT, THE UNDERSIGNED HEREBY ADOPTS THE FOLLOWING ARTICLES OF ORGANIZATION.

Article I   The name of the Limited Liability Company:

_____

(Your company title must end with the words Limited Liability Company, L.L.C. or LLC)

Article II   The duration of the Limited Liability Company is _____.

Article III   The Limited Liability Company has been organized for the following purpose(s):

_____

_____

Article IV   The **street address** (NO PO BOX) of the registered office:_____

_____ and the name of the

registered agent at that office:_____

Article V   The **names** and **addresses** of the initial member(s), and organizer (if any):

_____

_____

(Attach additional sheets if necessary.)

Article VI   If the Limited Liability Company is to be managed by one or more managers, list the names and addresses of the managers who are to serve until the first annual meeting of the members or until their successors are elected and qualified.

_____

_____

Any provision that is not inconsistent with the law for the regulation of the internal affairs of the Limited Liability Company is permitted to be set forth in the operating agreement of the LLC.

IN WITNESS THEREOF, the undersigned members executed these Articles of Organization on this the _____ day of _____, 20_____.

THIS DOCUMENT PREPARED BY:

_____

Signature of Member/Organizer

DLL 1.1 Rev. 6/2001

Alaska

Department of Commerce and Economic
Development
Division of B.S.C.
Attention: Corporation Section
P.O. Box 110808
Juneau, AK 99811-0808
907-465-2530
Fax: 907-465-3257

Website:
www.commerce.state.ak.us/bsc/home.htm

WHAT THEY SUPPLY:

General information on forming a LLC under the
Alaska Limited Liability Act, as well as instructions on
filing the Articles of Organization. State provides fill-
in-the-blank Articles of Organization form and the
Standard Industrial Classification (S.I.C.) code to
determine the LLC's purpose.

WHAT MUST BE FILED:

An original and an exact copy of the fill-in-the-blank
Articles of Organization. The Articles should contain a
statement that they are being filed under the provisions of the Alaska Limited Liability Act.

NAME REQUIREMENTS:

The name must contain the words "Limited Liability
Company" or the abbreviation "LLC." The name may
not contain the word "city" or "borough," or otherwise
imply that the company is a municipality. The name
must be distinguishable from trade names on record
with the Division of Banking, Securities, and
Corporations.

ARTICLES SPECIAL REQUIREMENTS:

The purpose of the LLC must be characterized with at
least two S.I.C. code numbers which are listed in the
chart on the next page.

FILING FEES:

The filing fee is $250 which includes a biennial license
fee of $100. The fee is payable to the "State of
Alaska."

REPORTS:

An LLC Company Report must be filed every two
years with a $100 biennial fee. The report must be
delivered before January 2nd of each year.

RECORDS REQUIRED:

- Names and addresses of members and managers
- Articles and all amendments
- Three years of financial records
- Three years of tax returns
- Operating agreement and all amendments

STATUTES:

Alaska Statutes, Title 10, beginning with Section 50.010,
Alaska Limited Liability Act.

ARTICLES OF ORGANIZATION
(Domestic Limited Liability Company)

The undersigned person(s) of the age of 18 years or more, acting as organizers of a limited liability company under the Alaska Limited Liability Act (AS 10.50) hereby adopt the following Articles of Organization:

ARTICLE I: Name of the Limited Liability Company. The name of a limited liability company must contain the words "limited liability company" or the abbreviation "L.L.C.," or "LLC".

ARTICLE 2: The purpose for which the company is organized. A limited liability company may list any lawful as its purpose.

ARTICLE 3: Registered Agent Name and Address.

Name			
Mailing Address			
Physical Address if Mailing Address is a Post Office Box			
City, State, Zip		AK	

ARTICLE 4: Duration:

Check this box if the duration is perpetual: ☐

If the duration is not perpetual, list the latest date upon which the Limited Liability Company is to dissolve:	

ARTICLE 5: Management: Check this box if the company will be managed by a manager. ☐

ARTICLE 6: Optional Provisions (Attach a separate 8 ½ X 11 sheet if necessary.)

One or more organizer shall sign the Articles of Organization for a limited liability company.

Name of Organizer (Print or Type)	Signature of Organizer
Name of Organizer (Print or Type)	Signature of Organizer
Date	Contact Name and Phone Number (To resolve questions with this filing)

Mail the application with **$250.00** and the Disclosure of Company Activities to:

**State of Alaska
Banking, Securities, and Corporations
Corporations Section
PO Box 110808, Juneau AK 99811-0808**

08-430 (Rev. 5/04 alh)

Arizona

Arizona Corporation Commission
1300 West Washington
Phoenix, AZ 85007-2929
602-542-3026
800-345-5819 (Arizona residents only)
or
400 West Congress
Tucson, AZ 85701-1347
520-628-6560

Website:
www.cc.state.az.us/corp/index.htm

WHAT THEY SUPPLY:

State provides duplicate filing package containing instructions, "filing checklist," and the Articles of Organization fill-in-the-blank form.

WHAT MUST BE FILED:

The original and one copy of the Articles of Organization must be filed with the Corporation Commission, copies will be returned if all requirements have been satisfied. DOMESTIC companies must publish a Notice of Filing. Within sixty days after filing, three consecutive publications of the Articles of Organization must be published in a newspaper of general circulation where the LLC has its place of business. Within ninety days after filing, an Affidavit evidencing the publication must also be filed with the Commission. This Affidavit will be supplied by the newspaper.

NAME REQUIREMENTS:

The name must contain the words "Limited Liability Company" or the abbreviations "L.L.C." or "L.C." You should check with the LLC filing office if the desired name is available. A name can be reserved for 120 days for a fee of $10. If you are a holder of a tradename or trademark that is identical or non-distinguishable from the proposed name, make sure you have a copy of the tradename certificate to attach to the Articles of Organization.

ARTICLES SPECIAL REQUIREMENTS:

The LLC must have a registered office and a statutory agent at a street address. The agent must sign the Articles or provide a consent to acceptance of appointment.

FILING FEES:

There is a $50 filing fee for Domestic LLCs and $150 for Foreign LLCs. Also, an expedited service is available for an additional $35 fee. Fees must be paid to the "Arizona Corporation Commission."

REPORTS:

Like a domestic corporation, the LLC must deliver to the commission for filing an annual report containing the basic information about the company and its financial condition. The annual filing fee is to be paid on or before the date assigned by the commission.

RECORDS REQUIRED:

- Names and addresses of members and managers
- Articles and all amendments
- Three years of financial records
- Three years of tax returns
- Operating agreement and all amendments

STATUTES:

Title 29, Chapter 4, Arizona Statutes (Arizona Limited Liability Company Act).

ARTICLES OF ORGANIZATION

A.R.S. §29-632

1.   <u>Name</u>. The name of the limited liability company is:

    _____

2.   <u>Known Place of Business</u>. The address of the company's known place of business in Arizona is:

    _____

    _____

3.   <u>Statutory Agent</u>. (In Arizona) The name and street address of the statutory agent of the company is:

    _____

    _____

    _____

Acceptance of Appointment By Statutory Agent

I _____, having been designated to act as
      (Printed Name)
Statutory Agent, hereby consent to act in that capacity until removed or resignation is submitted in accordance with the Arizona Revised Statutes.

_____

Signature of Statutory Agent

_____

   [If signing on behalf of a company serving as statutory agent, print company name here]

4.   <u>Dissolution</u>. The latest date, if any, on which the limited liability company must dissolve is:

    _____.

5. <u>Management</u>.

☐ Management of the limited liability company is **vested in a manager or managers.** The names and addresses of each person who is a manager <u>AND</u> each member who owns a twenty percent or greater interest in the capital or profits of the limited liability company are:

_____

[ ] member   [ ] manager

_____

_____

_____

[ ] member   [ ] manager

_____

_____

_____

[ ] member   [ ] manager

_____

_____

_____

[ ] member   [ ] manager

_____

_____

☐ Management of the limited liability company is **reserved to the members.** The names and addresses of each person who is a member are:

_____

[ ] member

_____

_____

_____

[ ] member

_____

_____

_____

[ ] member

_____

_____

_____

[ ] member

_____

_____

EXECUTED this _____ day of _____, _____.

_____   _____
            [Signature]   [Signature]

_____   _____
         [Print Name Here]   [Print Name Here]

PHONE _____   FAX _____

See A.R.S. §29-601 et seq. for more info.

Arkansas

Secretary of State
Corporation Division
State Capitol
Room 256
Little Rock, AR 72201
501-682-5078
888-233-0325 (outside of the Little Rock area)

Website:
www.sosweb.state.ar.us/corp_ucc_business.html

WHAT THEY SUPPLY:

State provides duplicate of fill-in-the-blank Articles of Organization form with instructions and an application for the franchise tax reporting form.

WHAT MUST BE FILED:

File two copies of Articles of Organization. A file stamped copy will be returned to you after filing has been completed. Also file one copy of Limited Liability Company Franchise Tax registration form.

NAME REQUIREMENTS:

The name must contain the words "Limited Liability Company" or the abbreviation "L.L.C.," "L.C.," "LLC," or "LC." Companies which perform professional service must additionally contain the words "Professional Limited Liability Company," or the abbreviations "P.L.L.C.," "P.L.C.," "PLLC," or "PLC."

An LLC name may be reserved for 120 days for a fee of $25.

ARTICLES SPECIAL REQUIREMENTS:

Registered agent must sign acknowledgment and acceptance of the appointment.

If the management of the company is vested in managers this must be stated in the articles.

FILING FEES:

There is a $50 filing fee for domestic companies, $300 for foreign LLCs.

REPORTS:

The annual report is due before June 1 each year. The filing fee is $109.

RECORDS REQUIRED:

- Names and addresses of members and managers
- Articles and all amendments
- Three years of financial records
- Three years of tax returns
- Operating agreement and all amendments

STATUTES:

Small Business Entity Tax Pass Through Act, Act 1003 of 1993, Ark. Code Annotated, beginning with Section 4-32-101.

Arkansas Secretary of State

Charlie Daniels

State Capitol • Little Rock, Arkansas 72201-1094
501-682-3409 • www.sosweb.state.ar.us

Instructions: File with the Secretary of State, State Capitol, Little Rock, Arkansas 72201-1094. A copy will be returned after filing has been completed.

PLEASE TYPE OR CLEARLY PRINT IN INK

ARTICLES OF ORGANIZATION

The undersigned authorized manager or member or person forming this Limited Liability Company under the Small Business Entity Tax Pass Through Act, Act 1003 of 1993, adopts the following Articles of Organization of such Limited Liability Company:

First: The Name of the Limited Liability Company is:

> Must contain the words "Limited Liability Company," "Limited Company," or the abbreviation "L.L.C.," "L.C.," "LLC," or "LC." The word "Limited" may be abbreviated as "Ltd.", and the word "Company" may be abbreviated as "Co." Companies which perform Professional Service MUST additionally contain the words "Professional Limited Liability Company," "Professional Limited Company," or the abbreviations "P.L.L.C.," "P.L.C.," "PLLC," or "PLC" and may not contain the name of a person who is not a member except that of a deceased member. The word "Limited" may be abbreviated as "Ltd." and the word "Company" may be abbreviated as "Co."

Second: Address of registered office of the Limited Liability Company which may be, but need not be, the place of business shall be:

_____

_____

_____

Third: The name of the registered agent and the physical business address of said agent shall be:

_____

_____

_____

(a) Acknowledgment and acceptance of appointment MUST be signed. I hereby acknowledge and accept the appointment of registered agent for and on behalf of the above named Limited Liability Company.

_____
Please sign here

Fourth: IF THE MANAGEMENT OF THIS COMPANY IS VESTED IN A MANAGER OR MANAGERS, A STATE-MENT TO THAT EFFECT MUST BE INCLUDED IN THE SPACE PROVIDED OR BY ATTACHMENT:

_____

PLEASE TYPE OR PRINT CLEARLY IN INK THE NAME OF THE PERSON (S) AUTHORIZED TO EXECUTE THIS DOCUMENT.

_____

Signature of authorized manager, member, or person forming this Company: _____

California

Secretary of State
Corporations Division
1500 11ᵗʰ Street
Sacramento, CA 95814
916-657-5448
or
Statement of Information Unit
(filings only)
P.O. Box 944230
Sacramento, CA 94244-2300

Website:
www.ss.ca.gov/business/business.htm

WHAT THEY SUPPLY:

State provides any fill-in-the-blank forms concerning the limited liability company with instructions and a fee schedule.

WHAT MUST BE FILED:

File only the original executed document together with the filing fee. A certified copy of the original document will be returned to you after filing.

NAME REQUIREMENTS:

The name must end with the words "Limited Liability Company," "Ltd. Liability Co.," or the abbreviation "LLC," or "L.L.C." as the last words. It must not be similar to a name of any other existing limited liability company. It may contain the name of one or two members, but may not contain the words "bank," "insurance," "trust," "corporation," or "incorporated."

For name reservation, file an application with the secretary of state with a $10 fee. If the desired name is available it will be reserved for a period of sixty days.

In California, you *cannot* form a professional limited liability company.

MEMBERS REQUIREMENTS:

Single member limited liability companies may now be formed.

ARTICLES SPECIAL REQUIREMENTS:

The Articles must be filed on California form LLC-1 and not a substitute. A form is on the next page.

FILING FEES:

There is a filing fee of $70, payable to the "Limited Liability Company Unit." However, see the other fees below.

REPORTS:

The annual minimum tax for "the privilege of doing business in California" is $800. You must pay this fee within three months after forming your LLC. If the total income of your LLC is more than $249,999, there's an additional fee of $500 and if it is over $499,999 the fee goes up in steps to $4,500 annually.

A tax voucher (form 3522) must be requested from the Franchise Tax Board. The toll-free number is 800-852-5711.

RECORDS REQUIRED:

- Names and addresses of members and managers
- Articles and all amendments
- Three years of financial records
- Six years of tax returns
- Operating agreement and all amendments

STATUTES:

California Corporation Code, Section 17000-17062 (Beverly-Killea Limited Liability Company Act).

State of California
Kevin Shelley
Secretary of State

File # _____

LIMITED LIABILITY COMPANY ARTICLES OF ORGANIZATION

A $70.00 filing fee must accompany this form.

IMPORTANT – Read instructions before completing this form.

This Space For Filing Use Only

ENTITY NAME (End the name with the words "Limited Liability Company," "Ltd. Liability Co.," or the abbreviations "LLC" or "L.L.C.")

1. NAME OF LIMITED LIABILITY COMPANY

PURPOSE (The following statement is required by statute and may not be altered.)

2. THE PURPOSE OF THE LIMITED LIABILITY COMPANY IS TO ENGAGE IN ANY LAWFUL ACT OR ACTIVITY FOR WHICH A LIMITED LIABILITY COMPANY MAY BE ORGANIZED UNDER THE BEVERLY-KILLEA LIMITED LIABILITY COMPANY ACT.

INITIAL AGENT FOR SERVICE OF PROCESS (If the agent is an individual, the agent must reside in California and both Items 3 and 4 must be completed. If the agent is a corporation, the agent must have on file with the California Secretary of State a certificate pursuant to Corporations Code section 1505 and Item 3 must be completed (leave Item 4 blank).

3. NAME OF INITIAL AGENT FOR SERVICE OF PROCESS

4. IF AN INDIVIDUAL, ADDRESS OF INITIAL AGENT FOR SERVICE OF PROCESS IN CALIFORNIA   CITY   STATE   ZIP CODE

CA

MANAGEMENT (Check only one)

5. THE LIMITED LIABILITY COMPANY WILL BE MANAGED BY:

ONE MANAGER

MORE THAN ONE MANAGER

ALL LIMITED LIABILITY COMPANY MEMBER(S)

ADDITIONAL INFORMATION

6. ADDITIONAL INFORMATION SET FORTH ON THE ATTACHED PAGES, IF ANY, IS INCORPORATED HEREIN BY THIS REFERENCE AND MADE A PART OF THIS CERTIFICATE.

EXECUTION

7. I DECLARE I AM THE PERSON WHO EXECUTED THIS INSTRUMENT, WHICH EXECUTION IS MY ACT AND DEED.

_____   _____
SIGNATURE OF ORGANIZER   DATE

_____
TYPE OR PRINT NAME OF ORGANIZER

RETURN TO (Enter the name and the address of the person or firm to whom a copy of the filed document should be returned.)

8. NAME

FIRM

ADDRESS

CITY/STATE/ZIP

LLC-1 (REV 12/2004)   APPROVED BY SECRETARY OF STATE

Colorado

Secretary of State
Business Division
1560 Broadway, Suite 200
Denver, CO 80202-5169
303-894-2200

Website:
www.sos.state.co.us/pubs/business/main.htm

WHAT THEY SUPPLY:

State provides single copy of fill-in-the-blank Articles of Organization form.

WHAT MUST BE FILED:

You must file the typed original and one copy of the Articles of Organization with the secretary of state. You need to include a self-addressed envelope.

NAME REQUIREMENTS:

The name must contain the words "Limited Liability Company" or the abbreviation "LLC" or "L.L.C." The word "Limited" may be abbreviated as "Ltd." the word company as "Co."

You can check name availability by calling the secretary of state. A name reservation can be made for a $10 fee for 120 days.

ARTICLES SPECIAL REQUIREMENTS:

No special requirements.

FILING FEES:

There is a fee of $50 for the regular filing (payable to the "Secretary of State"), an additional $50 is required for expedited service (filing within twenty-four hours).

REPORTS:

Every two years a report must be filed with a $25 fee.

RECORDS REQUIRED:

- Names and addresses of members and managers
- Articles and all amendments
- Three years of financial records
- Three years of tax returns
- Operating agreement and all amendments
- Minutes of meetings
- Members' contributions
- Members' right of termination

STATUTES:

Colorado Limited Liability Company Act, Colorado Revised Statutes, beginning with Section 7-80-101.

Connecticut

Secretary of State
Commercial Recording Division
30 Trinity Street
Hartford, CT 06106
860-509-6002
860-509-6001

Website:
www.sots.state.ct.us/Business/BusinessMain.html

WHAT THEY SUPPLY:

State provides fill-in-the-blank Articles of Organization form with instructions.

WHAT MUST BE FILED:

Single copy of Articles of Organization must be filed with the secretary of state. You will receive a mailing receipt. Copies are at additional charge (see below).

NAME REQUIREMENTS:

The name must contain the words "Limited Liability Company" or the abbreviation "L.L.C." The words "Limited" and "Company" may be abbreviated as "Ltd." and "Co."

For name availability check with the secretary of state. A name reservation can be made for 120 days for a fee of $30.

ARTICLES SPECIAL REQUIREMENTS:

Statutory agent must sign.

FILING FEES:

There is a filing fee of $60, payable to the "Secretary of State." For a certified copy add an extra $25 for each document. For an ordinary copy the fee is $20.

REPORTS:

Annual report required with fee of $10.

RECORDS REQUIRED:

- Names and addresses of members and managers
- Articles and all amendments
- Three years of financial records
- Three years of tax returns
- Operating agreement and all amendments
- Names of past members and managers
- Prior operating agreements
- Members' contributions
- Members' right of termination

STATUTES:

Connecticut Limited Liability Company Act, Pub. Act 93-267, Connecticut Statutes, Title 34.

ARTICLES OF ORGANIZATION
DOMESTIC LIMITED LIABILITY COMPANY
Office of the Secretary of the State
30 Trinity Street / P.O. Box 150470 / Hartford, CT 06115-0470 / Rev. 10/01/2004
See reverse for instructions

Space For Office Use Only	Filing Fee: $60.00

Please contact the Department of Revenue Services or your tax advisor as to any potential tax liability relating to your business.

1. NAME OF THE LIMITED LIABILITY COMPANY

2. NATURE OF BUSINESS TO BE TRANSACTED OR THE PURPOSES TO BE PROMOTED

3. PRINCIPAL OFFICE ADDRESS (See instructions for further details.)

4. APPOINTMENT OF STATUTORY AGENT FOR SERVICE OF PROCESS

Name of agent	Business address (P.O. Box is not acceptable)
	Residence address (P.O. Box is not acceptable)

Acceptance of appointment

_____
Signature of agent

5. MANAGEMENT

(Place a check mark next to the following statement *only* if it applies)

_____ The management of the limited liability company shall be vested in one or more managers.

6. MANAGER(S) OR MEMBER(S) INFORMATION

Name	Title	Business Address	Residence Address

7. EXECUTION

Print or type name of organizer	Signature

Reference an 8 ½ x 11 attachment if additional space is required

Delaware

State of Delaware
Division of Corporations
John G. Townsend Building
401 Federal Street, Suite 4
Dover, DE 19901
    or (for regular mail)
P.O. Box 898
Dover, DE 19903
302-739-3073

Website:
www.state.de.us/corp

WHAT THEY SUPPLY:

State provides complete booklet about how to form a business in Delaware. This contains fill-in-the-blank Certificate of Formation, fee schedules, a franchise tax schedule, phone and fax directory, a list of registered agents, and other important information.

WHAT MUST BE FILED:

The original and one copy of the Certificate of Formation must be filed with the secretary of state. The documents must be submitted in the U.S. letter size (8.5"x11") with certain margins and must be either typed, printed, or written in black ink.

NAME REQUIREMENTS:

The name must contain the words "Limited Liability Company" or the abbreviation "L.L.C."

A name can be reserved for 120 days for a fee of $75.

ARTICLES SPECIAL REQUIREMENTS:

The document is called a "Certificate of Formation" in Delaware and has only three requirements, the name, address of the registered office, and name of registered agent.

FILING FEES:

The initial filing fee is $90, payable to the "Division of Corporations." Certified copies can be received for an additional $20 each. The Corporations' Division accepts major credit cards.

REPORTS:

Annual reports are required with a filing fee of $100 by June 1.

RECORDS REQUIRED:

- None required by statute

STATUTES:

Title 6, Commerce and Trade, Chapter 18, Limited Liability Company Act.

STATE *of* DELAWARE
LIMITED LIABILITY COMPANY
CERTIFICATE *of* FORMATION

- **First:** The name of the limited liability company is _____
_____

- **Second:** The address of its registered office in the State of Delaware is _____
_____ in the City of _____. The
name of its Registered agent at such address is _____
_____

- **Third:** (Use this paragraph only if the company is to have a specific effective date of
dissolution: "The latest date on which the limited liability company is to dissolve is
_____.")

- **Fourth:** (Insert any other matters the members determine to include herein.)
_____
_____
_____
_____
_____
_____
_____

In Witness Whereof, the undersigned have executed this Certificate of Formation this
_____ day of _____, 20_____.

By:_____
Authorized Person(s)

Name:_____
Typed or Printed

District of Columbia

Department of Consumer and Regulatory Affairs
Corporation Division
941 North Capital Street NE
Washington, D.C. 20002
202-442-4400

Website:
http://dcra.dc.gov/dcra/site/default.asp

WHAT THEY SUPPLY:

Office provides a sample of Articles of Organization (but no forms) with instructions on how to draft your own document. A blank form of a written consent of the registered agent is included.

WHAT MUST BE FILED:

You must file two signed originals of Articles of Organization. Attach the written consent of the registered agent.

NAME REQUIREMENTS:

The name must contain the words "Limited Liability Company" or the abbreviation "L.L.C." A name may be reserved for sixty days for $25. If your company is going to perform professional service, the name must contain the words "Professional Limited Liability Company."

ARTICLES SPECIAL REQUIREMENTS:

The registered agent must consent to his appointment.

If a general or limited partnership converts to a limited liability company, the former name and fact of conversion must be stated Articles of Organization.

FILING FEES:

There is a filing fee of $150 for a domestic LLC, payable to the "D.C. Treasurer."

REPORTS:

Annual report due every other year by June 16th, starting the first year after organizing, with $150 fee.

RECORDS REQUIRED:

- Names and addresses of members and managers
- Articles and all amendments
- Three years of financial records
- Three years of tax returns
- Operating agreement and all amendments

STATUTES:

Title 29, Chapter 10 of the District of Columbia Code (D.C. Limited Liability Company Act of 1994).

Government
of the
District of Columbia

DEPARTMENT OF CONSUMER AND REGULATORY AFFAIRS
BUSINESS AND PROFESSIONAL LICENSING ADMINISTRATION
CORPORATIONS DIVISION
941 NORTH CAPITOL STREET, N.E.
WASHINGTON, D.C. 20002

SAMPLE FORMAT FOR THE ARTICLES OF CORRECTION
TO THE
ARTICLES OF ORGANIZATION
OF A LIMITED LIABILITY COMPANY

NOTE: THIS IS ONLY A SPECIMEN. YOU MUST DRAFT YOUR OWN ARTICLES ON PLAIN BOND PAPER AND SUBMIT THEM IN **DUPLICATE ORIGINAL** (TWO MANUALLY SIGNED SETS) TO THE SUPERINTENDENT OF CORPORATIONS OF THE DISTRICT OF COLUMBIA ("SUPERINTENDENT OF CORPORATIONS")

DO NOT SIMPLY FILL IN THIS SPECIMEN.

A limited liability company may propose to correct its articles of organization if they contain typographical errors, errors of execution, errors of transcription or other technical errors. Articles of correction may not make any substantive amendment or change the effective date of the articles or organization.

ARTICLES OF CORRECTION
TO THE
ARTICLES OF ORGANIZATION

Pursuant to provisions of Title 29, Chapter 10 of the District of Columbia Code the D.C. Limited Liability Company Act of 1994, the undersigned limited liability company adopts the following Articles of Correction to its Articles of Organization:

FIRST: The name of the limited liability company is [insert the name of the company].
SECOND: The date the Articles of Organization were filed is [insert the date of filing].
THIRD: The following Correction to the Articles of Organization was adopted by the company on _____, 20___ in accordance with the Articles of Organization, Operating Agreement and all applicable laws of the District of Columbia: (State the provision in the articles of organization as previously filed and as corrected, and if execution of the articles of organization was defective, the manner in which it was defective).
FOURTH: The effective date of this correction shall be [insert this date, which maybe on or after the date of delivery for filing with the Superintendent of Corporations].
(**NOTE:** If accepted for filing, the effective date of the articles of correction will be the date of delivery unless the articles specify a later date.)
FIFTH: Choose A or B, with any appropriate deletions or insertions.
(A) The Correction was approved by those members with voting rights holding at least a majority of the interest in profits of the limited liability company.

(B) In accordance with the Articles of Organization and/or the Operating Agreement of the company, the Correction was approved by [describe any specified method of approval which does not involve approval by those members with voting rights holding at least a majority of the interest in profits of the company].

Date _____ 20____

_____

identify the limited liability company

BY:

_____

use a separate signature line for each authorized person required to participate in executing the Articles of Correction pursuant to applicable provisions of the company's governing document

MAIL TO:
DEPARTMENT OF CONSUMER AND REGULATORY AFFAIRS
BUSINESS AND PROFESSIONAL LICENSING ADMINISTRATION
CORPORATIONS DIVISION
941 NORTH CAPITOL STREET, N.E.
WASHINGTON, D.C. 20002
202-442-4432

FEES DUE
Filing Fee $150
Make Check Payable to D.C. Treasurer

Florida

Secretary of State
Division of Corporations
P.O. Box 6327
Tallahassee, FL 32314
800-755-5111

Website:
www.dos.state.fl.us/doc/index.html

WHAT THEY SUPPLY:

State provides complete filing package, including a booklet "Florida Limited Liability Company Act," a "Fictitious Name Registration Packet," a fill-in-the-blank Articles of Organization form, and complete instructions.

WHAT MUST BE FILED:

Unless this material has been included in your articles, one original copy of the Articles of Organization must be filed along with the Certificate of Designation of Registered Agent. An Affidavit of Membership and Contributions must also be filed unless this information is included in your articles. If you include a copy of the articles, it will be date-stamped and returned. Otherwise, you will receive an acknowledgement letter.

NAME REQUIREMENTS:

The company name must end with the words "Limited Liability Company" or "Limited Company" or the abbreviation "L.L.C." or "L.C." The name may not contain language implying that the LLC is connected with a state or federal government agency. It must be distinguishable from other company names already on file.

For name availability, check the Florida Website at **www.dos.state.fl.us**.

ARTICLES SPECIAL REQUIREMENTS:

If the Limited Liability Company is to be managed by one or more managers, a statement that the company is to be a manager-managed company needs to be included in the Articles.

An acceptance by the registered agent and an affidavit of membership and contributions must be either included in the Articles or on a separate form.

FILING FEES:

There is a filing fee of $100 for the Articles of Organization and the Affidavit plus an additional $25 for the Certificate of Designation of the registered agent. For another (optional) fee of $30, you can get a certified copy of the Articles. Make the check with the minimum fee ($125) payable to the "Florida Department of State."

REPORTS:

An annual report must be filed between January 1 and May 1 of each year with the annual fee of $50. If you fail to file the annual report in time, there is a $400 late fee.

RECORDS REQUIRED:

- Names and addresses of members
- Articles and all amendments
- Three years of financial records
- Three years of tax returns
- Operating agreement and all amendments
- Members' contributions

STATUTES:

Title 36, Chapter 608, Florida Statutes (Florida Limited Liability Company Act).

AUTHOR'S NOTE: *As this books goes to press, major revisions of the Florida Act are pending before the legislature.*

ARTICLES OF ORGANIZATION FOR FLORIDA LIMITED LIABILITY COMPANY

ARTICLE I - Name:

The name of the Limited Liability Company is:

_____

ARTICLE II - Address:

The mailing address and street address of the principal office of the Limited Liability Company is:

Principal Office Address: **Mailing Address:**

_____   _____

_____   _____

_____   _____

ARTICLE III - Registered Agent, Registered Office, & Registered Agent's Signature:

The name and the Florida street address of the registered agent are:

_____
Name

_____
Florida street address (P.O. Box **NOT** acceptable)

_____FL_____
City, State, and Zip

Having been named as registered agent and to accept service of process for the above stated limited liability company at the place designated in this certificate, I hereby accept the appointment as registered agent and agree to act in this capacity. I further agree to comply with the provisions of all statutes relating to the proper and complete performance of my duties, and I am familiar with and accept the obligations of my position as registered agent as provided for in Chapter 608, F.S..

_____
Registered Agent's Signature

(CONTINUED)

Page 1 of 2

ARTICLE IV- Manager(s) or Managing Member(s):
The name and address of each Manager or Managing Member is as follows:

<u>Title:</u>	<u>Name and Address:</u>
"MGR" = Manager	
"MGRM" = Managing Member	

_____

_____

_____

_____

(Use attachment if necessary)

NOTE: An additional article must be added if an effective date is requested.

REQUIRED SIGNATURE:

_____

Signature of a member or an authorized representative of a member.

(In accordance with section 608.408(3), Florida Statutes, the execution
of this document constitutes an affirmation under the penalties of perjury
that the facts stated herein are true.)

_____

Typed or printed name of signee

<u>**Filing Fees:**</u>

**$125.00 Filing Fee for Articles of Organization and Designation
        of Registered Agent**
$ 30.00 Certified Copy (Optional)
$ 5.00 Certificate of Status (Optional)

Page 2 of 2

Georgia

Secretary of State
2 Martin Luther King, Jr. Drive, S.E.
Suite 315, West Tower
Atlanta, GA 30334
404-656-2817

Website:
www.sos.state.ga.us/corporations

WHAT THEY SUPPLY:

State provides instructions for filing self-drafted Articles of Organization and gives a sample form containing the minimum of two Articles. Also a Transmittal Form is provided which must be filed with the Articles of Organization.

WHAT MUST BE FILED:

You must file the original and one copy of the Articles of Organization and attach the Transmittal form provided by the State.

NAME REQUIREMENTS:

The name must contain the words "Limited Liability Company" or "Limited Company" or the abbreviation "L.L.C." or "LLC."

A name should be reserved prior to filing. The reservation can be made at the website, **www.georgiacorporations.org**, or by faxing a request to (404) 651-7842. Reservations are not available by telephone.

If your proposed name is available, you will be mailed a reservation certificate with a reservation number that remains in effect for ninety days. The reservation number must be placed in the Transmittal Form that is filed with your Articles of Organization.

ARTICLES SPECIAL REQUIREMENTS:

The name of the company must be in the Articles. If the company is to be managed by someone other than the members, a clause should be added indicating who are the managers. Other information, such as the address of the company and registered agent, is to be included on the "Transmittal Information" sheet.

The Articles must be signed by all members.

FILING FEES:
There is a filing fee of $100, payable to the "Secretary of State."

REPORTS:

Annual report due before April 1st with $25 filing fee.

RECORDS REQUIRED:

- Names and addresses of members and managers
- Articles and all amendments
- Three years of financial records
- Three years of tax returns
- Operating agreement and all amendments

STATUTES:

Title 14, Chapter 11 of the Official Code of Georgia Annotated.

Hawaii

Business Registration Division
Department of Commerce
and Consumer Affairs
P.O. Box 40
Honolulu, HI 96810
808-586-2744

Website:
www.hawaii.gov/dcca

WHAT THEY SUPPLY:

State provides instructions and blank forms.

WHAT MUST BE FILED:

You must file the original and one copy of the Articles of Organization.

NAME REQUIREMENTS:

The name must contain the words "Limited Liability Company" or "Limited Company" or the abbreviation "L.L.C." or "LLC."

The abbreviations "Ltd." and "Co." can be used.

ARTICLES SPECIAL REQUIREMENTS:

The Articles should state that the members are not liable for the debts of the company under Section 428-303(c) Hawaii Statutes.

If there are managers their names and residence addresses must be included, otherwise the name and residence addresses of the members must be listed.

FILING FEES:

There is a filing fee of $100, payable to the "Department of Commerce and Consumer Affairs." Reviewing time is approximately twenty-two days unless you pay an additional $50.

REPORTS:

Annual report with $25 filing fee. The report is due before June 30 every year. The forms will be mailed to you before that date.

RECORDS REQUIRED:

- Names and addresses of members and managers
- Articles and all amendments
- Three years of financial records
- Three years of tax returns
- Operating agreement and all amendments
- Past members and managers

STATUTES:

Title 23A, Chapter 428, Hawaii Revised Statutes.

www.BusinessRegistrations.com

Nonrefundable Filing Fee: $50.00

FORM LLC-1

1/2005

STATE OF HAWAII
DEPARTMENT OF COMMERCE AND CONSUMER AFFAIRS
Business Registration Division
335 Merchant Street
Mailing Address: P.O. Box 40, Honolulu, Hawaii 96810

ARTICLES OF ORGANIZATION FOR LIMITED LIABILITY COMPANY
(Section 428-203, Hawaii Revised Statutes)

PLEASE TYPE OR PRINT LEGIBLY IN BLACK INK

The undersigned, for the purpose of forming a limited liability company under the laws of the State of Hawaii, do hereby make and execute these Articles of Organization:

I

The name of the company shall be:

_____

(The name must contain the words *Limited Liability Company* or the *abbreviation L.L.C. or LLC*)

II

The mailing address of the initial principal office is:

_____

III

The company shall have and continuously maintain in the State of Hawaii an agent and street address of the agent for service of process on the company. The agent may be an individual resident of Hawaii, a domestic entity, or a foreign entity authorized to transact or conduct affairs in this State, whose business office is identical with the registered office.

a.   The name of the company's initial agent for service of process is:

_____   _____
(Name of Registered Agent)   (State or Country)

b.   The street address of the initial registered office in this State is:

_____

IV

The name and address of each organizer is:

_____   _____

_____   _____

_____   _____

_____   _____

V

The period of duration is (check one):

[ ] At-will

[ ] For a specified term to expire on: _____
                             (Month)   (Day)   (Year)

VI

The company is (check one):

[ ] Manager-managed, and the names and addresses of the initial managers are listed below.

    (Number of initial members: _____)

[ ] Member-managed, and the names and addresses of the initial members are listed below.

_____   _____

_____   _____

_____   _____

_____   _____

_____   _____

VII

The members of the company (check one):

[ ] Shall not be liable for the debts, obligations and liabilities of the company.

[ ] Shall be liable for some or all, *as stated below*, of the specified debts, obligations and liabilities of the company, and have consented in writing to the adoption of this provision or to be bound by this provision.

_____

_____

We certify, under the penalties set forth in the Hawaii Uniform Limited Liability Company Act, that we have read the above statements and that the same are true and correct.

Signed this _____day of _____, _____

_____   _____
    (Type/Print Name of Organizer)   (Type/Print Name of Organizer)

_____   _____
     (Signature of Organizer)   (Signature of Organizer)

SEE INSTRUCTIONS PAGE. The articles must be signed and certified by at least one organizer of the company.

Idaho

Secretary of State
Attn: Commercial Division
P.O. Box 83720
Boise, ID 83720-0080
208-334-2301

Website:
www.idsos.state.id.us/corp/corindex.htm

WHAT THEY SUPPLY:

State provides two fill-in-the-blank Articles of Organization forms with instructions and, on request, a booklet containing the Limited Liability Company Act.

WHAT MUST BE FILED:

You must file two completed originals. The fill-in-the-blank forms must be typed, if not typed or if the attachments are not included, there is an additional $20 fee for filing.

If you have questions about the correct filing, you can call the secretary of state's office at 208-334-2301.

NAME REQUIREMENTS:

The name must contain the words "Limited Liability Company" or the abbreviation "L.L.C." or "L.C." The word "Limited" may be abbreviated as "Ltd.," and the word "Company" as "Co."

If you want to perform professional services, the company's name must end with the words "Professional Company" or the abbreviation "P.L.L.C." or "PLLC."

A name may be reserved for $20 for four months.

ARTICLES SPECIAL REQUIREMENTS:

The address of the registered office may not be a P.O. Box, but must be a physical address in Idaho. The registered agent must sign the articles. If the management shall be vested in managers, at least one manager has to sign the Articles.

The name and address of at least one manager or member must be included.

FILING FEES:

There is a filing fee of $100, payable to the "Idaho Secretary of State." If the articles are not typed or if there are attachments, there is an additional $20 fee. Expedited service is an additional $20.

REPORTS:

The annnual report shall be delivered to the secretary of state each year before the end of the month during which your company was initially organized, beginning one year after it is organized.

RECORDS REQUIRED:

- Names and addresses of members and managers
- Articles and all amendments
- Three years of financial records
- Three years of tax returns
- Operating agreement and all amendments
- Past members and managers

STATUTES:

Title 53, Chapter 6, Idaho Limited Liability Company Act.

ARTICLES OF ORGANIZATION
LIMITED LIABILITY COMPANY

(Instructions on back of application)

1. The name of the limited liability company is:

    _____

2. The street address of the initial registered office is:

    _____

    and the name of the initial registered agent at the above address is:

    _____

3. The mailing address for future correspondence is:

    _____

4. Management of the limited liability company will be vested in:

    Manager(s) ☐ or Member(s) ☐   (please check the appropriate box)

5. If management is to be vested in one or more manager(s), list the name(s) and address(es) of at least one initial manager. If management is to be vested in the member(s), list the name(s) and address(es) of at least one initial member.

Name	Address
_____	_____
_____	_____
_____	_____
_____	_____
_____	_____
_____	_____

6. Signature of at least one person responsible for forming the limited liability company:

    Signature: _____

    Typed Name: _____

    Capacity: _____

    Signature _____

    Typed Name: _____

    Capacity: _____

g:\corp\forms\LLC forms\artsoforganization.p65
Revised 07/2002

Secretary of State use only

Illinois

Springfield Office:

Secretary of State
Business Services Dept.
Michael J. Howlett Bldg.
501 S. 2nd Street
Room 328
Springfield, IL 62756
217-782-6961

Chicago Office:

Secretary of State
Business Services Dept.
69 W. Washington
Suite 1240
Chicago, IL 60602
312-793-3380

Website:
www.cyberdriveillinois.com/departments/
business_services/home.html

WHAT THEY SUPPLY:

State provides complete filing package, including numerous forms, booklets "The Illinois Limited Liability Company Act" and "Limited Liability Corporations," a name fee schedule, phone directory, and a Business Activity Code which is similar to the Standard Industrial Code (SIC).

WHAT MUST BE FILED:

File the original and one copy of the signed Articles of Organization form. The form must be typed.

NAME REQUIREMENTS:

The company's name must contain the words "Limited Liability Company," "L.L.C.," or "LLC," but may not contain the terms "Ltd.," "Co.," "Inc.," "Corporation," "Corp.," "Incorporated," "Partnership," or "LP." It must be distinguishable from other company names already on file.

A name may be reserved using a special Reservation form (included in the filing package) for a $300 fee. We suggest to just check the name availability under 217-782-9520 if a reservation is not essential.

ARTICLES SPECIAL REQUIREMENTS:

If there are managers, their names and residence addresses must be included; otherwise the name and residence addresses of the members must be listed.

In Article 6 you are asked for the business purpose by (SIC) code. However, the statute states that the purpose can be "any or all lawful business."

FILING FEES:

The fee is $400, and must be made by a certified check, cashier's check, Illinois attorney's check, or money order, payable to "Secretary of State."

REPORTS:

The annual report must be delivered to the secretary of state before the first day of the anniversary month. The annual fee is $200. If you fail to file the report within another sixty day period after the first day of the anniversary month, there will be a penalty of $100.

RECORDS REQUIRED:

- Names, addresses and dates of members
- Articles and all amendments
- Three years of financial records
- Three years of tax returns
- Operating agreement and all amendments
- Members' contributions

STATUTES:

The Illinois Limited Liability Company Act, 805 ILCS 180.

Form **LLC-5.5** December 2003	**Illinois** **Limited Liability Company Act** **Articles of Organization**	This space for use by Secretary of State

Jesse White
Secretary of State
Department of Business Services
Limited Liability Company Division
Room 351, Howlett Building
Springfield, IL 62756
http://www.cyberdriveillinois.com

SUBMIT IN DUPLICATE
Must be typewritten

This space for use by Secretary of State

Payment must be made by certified check, cashier's check, Illinois attorney's check, Illinois C.P.A.'s check or money order, payable to "Secretary of State."

Date
Assigned File #
Filing Fee $500.00
Approved:

1. Limited Liability Company Name: _____

   _____
   (The LLC name must contain the words limited liability company, L.L.C. or LLC and cannot contain the terms corporation, corp., incorporated, inc., ltd., co., limited partnership, or L.P.)

2. The address of its principal place of business: (Post office box alone and c/o are unacceptable.)

   _____

   _____ .

3. The Articles of Organization are effective on: (Check one)

   a) _____ the filing date, or b) _____ another date later than but not more than 60 days subsequent
   to the filing date: _____
   (month, day, year)

4. The registered agent's name and registered office address is:

   Registered agent: _____
   First Name   *Middle Initial*   *Last Name*

   Registered Office:
   (P.O. Box and   _____
   c/o are unacceptable)   *Number*   *Street*   *Suite #*

   _____
   City   *ZIP Code*   *County*

5. Purpose or purposes for which the LLC is organized: Include the business code # (IRS Form 1065).
   (If not sufficient space to cover this point, add one or more sheets of this size.)

   "The transaction of any or all lawful business for which limited liability companies may be organized under this Act."

6. The latest date, if any, upon which the company is to dissolve _____ .
   (month, day, year)

   Any other events of dissolution enumerated on an attachment. (Optional)

LLC-5.5

7. Other provisions for the regulation of the internal affairs of the LLC per Section 5-5 (a) (8) included as attachment:

    If yes, state the provisions(s) from the ILLCA.   ☐ Yes   ☐ No

8. a) Management is by manager(s):   ☐ Yes   ☐ No
    If yes, list names and business addresses.

    b) Management is vested in the member(s):   ☐ Yes   ☐ No
    If yes, list names and addresses.

9. I affirm, under penalties of perjury, having authority to sign hereto, that these articles of organization are to the best of my knowledge and belief, true, correct and complete.

    Dated _____ , _____
                    (Month/Day)   (Year)

Signature(s) and Name(s) of Organizer(s)   **Address(es)**

1. _____   1. _____
           Signature   *Number*   *Street*

   _____   _____
     (Type or print name and title)   *City/Town*

   _____   _____
   (Name if a corporation or other entity)   *State*   *ZIP Code*

2. _____   2. _____
           Signature   *Number*   *Street*

   _____   _____
     (Type or print name and title)   *City/Town*

   _____   _____
   (Name if a corporation or other entity)   *State*   *ZIP Code*

3. _____   3. _____
           Signature   *Number*   *Street*

   _____   _____
     (Type or print name and title)   *City/Town*

   _____   _____
   (Name if a corporation or other entity)   *State*   *ZIP Code*

(Signatures must be in ink on an original document. Carbon copy, photocopy or rubber stamp signatures may only be used on conformed copies.)

Indiana

Secretary of State
302 W. Washington, Room E018
Indianapolis, IN 46204
317-232-6576

Website:
www.in.gov/sos/business/index.html

WHAT THEY SUPPLY:

State provides instructions how to draft your own Articles of Organization, it also includes a fee schedule and instructions on how to download forms from their website.

WHAT MUST BE FILED:

File original and two copies of the Articles of Organization with the secretary of state. Enclose the filing fee.

NAME REQUIREMENTS:

The company name must contain the words "Limited Liability Company," "L.L.C.," or "LLC." It must be distinguishable from other companies already on file. You can get a name reservation for 120 days for a $20 fee. For availability, you can check by phone.

ARTICLES SPECIAL REQUIREMENTS:

No unusual clauses are required.

FILING FEES:

There is a filing fee of $90, payable to the "Secretary of State."

REPORTS:

Annual report must be filed with $30 filing fee. The report is due in the anniversary month of the company every two years. If your company was organized in an odd year, you need to report every odd year, and if it was organized in an even year, your report needs to be filed every even year.

RECORDS REQUIRED:

- Names and addresses of members and managers
- Articles and all amendments
- Three years of financial records
- Three years of tax returns
- Operating agreement and all amendments

STATUTES:

Indiana Code Title 23, Chapter 18.

Iowa

Secretary of State
Corporations Division
Lucas Building, 1st Floor
321 East 12th Street
Des Moines, IA 50319
515-281-5204

Website:
www.sos.state.ia.us/business

WHAT THEY SUPPLY:

State provides a copy of the law, but no forms. In section 490A.303, you will find the requirements for the Articles of Organization.

WHAT MUST BE FILED:

File only the original of your Articles of Organization. The document must be typed or printed in black ink. If all requirements are met, the Articles will be returned as filed.

NAME REQUIREMENTS:

The company name must contain the words "Limited Company" or the abbreviation " L.C.," but may not contain the words "Corporation," "Incorporated," "Corp." or the like. It must be distinguishable from company names already on file.

For a $10 fee you can reserve a name for 120 days.

ARTICLES SPECIAL REQUIREMENTS:

The principal office must be listed. (This may be the same as the registered office, but doesn't need to be.)

FILING FEES:

There is a filing fee of $50, payable to the "Secretary of State."

REPORTS:

No annual reporting fee.

RECORDS REQUIRED:

- Names and addresses of members and managers
- Articles and all amendments
- Three years of financial records
- Three years of tax returns
- Operating agreement and all amendments

STATUTES:

Chapter 490A, Iowa Codes, Iowa Limited Liability Company Act.

Kansas

Secretary of State
Corporation Division
Memorial Hall, 1st Floor
120 SW 10th Avenue
Topeka, KS 66612-1594
785-296-4564

Website:
www.kssos.org/business/business.html

WHAT THEY SUPPLY:

State provides one copy of fill-in-the-blank Articles of Organization with instructions.

WHAT MUST BE FILED:

The Articles of Organization must be signed by the person forming the organization or by any member or manager. You must file the original signed copy and one duplicate, which may either be a signed or conformed copy. Enclose the filing fee.

NAME REQUIREMENTS:

The company name must contain the words "Limited Company" or the abbreviations "L.C." or "LC," or the words "Limited Liability Company" or the abbreviations "L.L.C." or "LLC." The name must be distinguishable from other entity names in Kansas.

ARTICLES SPECIAL REQUIREMENTS:

The address of its registered office and the address of the registered agent for service of process must be the same, but the agent can be the LLC itself.

If the members have the right to admit additional members, this must be included in the Articles along with the terms and conditions of the admission.

If the remaining members have the right to continue the business upon any event which terminates the continued membership of a member of the limited liability company, this must be included.

The names and addresses of the managers or if none, names and addresses of the members must be included.

FILING FEES:

There is a filing fee of $165, payable to the "Secretary of State."

REPORTS:

Annual report with a minimum of $25 fee. The report is due the fifteenth day of the fourth month following the close of your company's fiscal year.

RECORDS REQUIRED:

- Names and addresses of members and managers
- Articles and all amendments
- Three years of financial records
- Three years of tax returns
- Minutes and resolutions

STATUTES:

Kansas Statutes Annotated, beginning with Section 17-7601.

KANSAS SECRETARY OF STATE
Kansas Limited Liability Company **DL**
Articles of Organization
51

All information must be completed or this document will not be accepted for filing.

1. Name of the limited liability company (must include "limited liability company," "limited company," "LLC" or "LC"):

_____

2. Name and address of resident agent and registered office in Kansas:
Address must be a street address. A post office box is unacceptable.

Do not write in this space

Name	Street address	City	State	Zip

PROFESSIONAL LIMITED LIABILITY COMPANIES ONLY: *(See instruction below)*

If the LLC is organized to exercise the powers of a professional association, state the professional purpose of the LLC:

_____

_____

If the LLC is organized to exercise powers of a professional association or corporation, the LLC must file a certificate from the licensing board of the profession, stating that each LLC member is duly licensed to practice that profession and that the proposed company name has been approved. The following professions are authorized to create a professional LLC: architect, attorney-at-law, certified public accountant, chiropractor, clinical marriage and family therapist, clinical professional counselor, clinical psychotherapist, dentist, engineer, geologist, land surveyor, landscape architect, licensed psychologist, occupational therapist, optometrist, osteopathic physician or surgeon, pharmacist, physician, physician assistant, surgeon or doctor of medicine, podiatrist, real estate broker or salesperson, registered physical therapist, registered professional nurse, specialist in clinical social work, veterinarian.

I declare under penalty of perjury under the laws of the state of Kansas that the foregoing is true and correct.

Executed on the _____ of _____ , _____ .
                      Day   Month   Year

_____
Organizer

LLC Mailing Information

Where would you like the Secretary of State's office to send official mail? If no address is given, the mail will be sent to the LLC's registered office.

Street address	City	State	Zip	Country

The mail should be addressed to the following named individual: _____

Instruction
   Submit this form with the $165 filing fee.

Notice: There is a $25 service fee for all returned checks.

Kentucky

Commonwealth of Kentucky
Office of the Secretary of State
700 Capitol Avenue, Suite 152
Frankfort, KY 40601
502-564-3490

Website:
www.sos.state.ky.us

WHAT THEY SUPPLY:

State provides fill-in-the-blank Articles of Organization and filing instructions.

WHAT MUST BE FILED:

File your typewritten (or printed) and signed Articles original accompanied by two exact copies. If the company will be managed by managers, the documents must be signed by the managers, or by a least one member. The person signing the document has to state the capacity in which she or he signs.

NAME REQUIREMENTS:

The name must contain the words "Limited Liability Company," or "Limited Company," or the abbreviations "LLC" or "LC." The word "Limited" may be abbreviated as "Ltd." and the word "Company" as "Co."

Professional LLCs must contain the words "Professional Limited Company" or "Professional Limited Liability Company" or the abbreviation "PLLC" or "PLC."

The name must be distinguishable from any other name on record with the secretary of state. You can check the name availability by calling 502-564-2848. A name can be reserved for a $15 fee for a period of 120 days.

ARTICLES SPECIAL REQUIREMENTS:

The registered agent must consent to his or her appointment by signing the Articles.

FILING FEES:

There is a filing fee of $40 payable to the "Kentucky State Treasurer."

REPORTS:

The first annual report must be delivered to the secretary of state between January 1 and June 30 of the year following the calendar year in which the company was organized. Reports are due June 30 in each subsequent year. The annual fee is $15.

RECORDS REQUIRED:

- Names and addresses of members and managers
- Articles and all amendments
- Three years of financial records
- Three years of tax returns
- Operating agreement and all amendments

STATUTES:

Chapter 275 Kentucky Statutes, Kentucky Limited Liability Company Act.

COMMONWEALTH OF KENTUCKY
TREY GRAYSON
SECRETARY OF STATE

ARTICLES OF ORGANIZATION
Limited Liability Company

For the purposes of forming a limited liability company in Kentucky pursuant to KRS Chapter 275, the undersigned organizer(s) hereby submit(s) the following Articles of Organization to the Secretary of State for filing:

Article I: The name of the limited liability company is

_____.

Article II: The street address of the limited liability company's initial registered office in Kentucky is

_____
Street   City   State   Zip Code

and the name of the initial registered agent at that office is _____.

Article III: The mailing address of the limited liability company's initial principal office is

_____
Street or PO Box Number   City   State   Zip Code

Article IV: The limited liability company is to be managed by:

      a manager or managers.
                           (must check one)
      its member(s).

Executed by the Organizer(s) on _____

Date

_____
Signature of Organizer

_____
Type or Print Name of Organizer

_____
Signature of Organizer

_____
Type or Pint Name of Organizer

I, _____, consent to serve as the registered agent on behalf of the company.
Type or print name of registered agent

_____
Signature of Registered Agent

_____
Type or Print Name & Title

Louisiana

Secretary of State
Corporations Division
P.O. Box 94125
Baton Rouge, LA 70804-9125
225-925-4704

Website:
www.sos.louisiana.gov/comm/corp/corp-index.htm

WHAT THEY SUPPLY:

State provides fill-in-the-blank Articles of Organization and a "Limited Liability Company Initial Report" that contains the agent's affidavit and acknowledgment of acceptance. Both forms come with instructions. For a fee of $10, you can receive a "Corporation Laws" booklet which covers LLC laws.

WHAT MUST BE FILED:

Complete both the Articles and the Initial Report. Both documents must be signed by the people organizing the LLC and both must be notarized. File only the originals and enclose the filing fee.

NAME REQUIREMENTS:

Your company name must contain the words "Limited Liability Company" or the abbreviation "L.L.C." or "L.C."

Names can be reserved for a fee of $20 for sixty days.

ARTICLES SPECIAL REQUIREMENTS:

Articles of Organization must be notarized. They must be accompanied by form 973 "Initial Report" which must be signed by all persons who signed the Articles of Organization and the registered agent and be notarized.

FILING FEES:

There is a filing fee of $75, payable to the "Secretary of State."

REPORTS:

Annual report required with $75 filing fee. The report is due on the anniversary date of the organization. The forms will be mailed to you one month prior to the due date.

RECORDS REQUIRED:

- Names and addresses of members and managers
- Articles and all amendments
- Three years of financial records
- Three years of tax returns
- Operating agreement and all amendments

STATUTES:

Louisiana Revised Statutes beginning with Section 12:1301.

W. FOX McKEITHEN
SECRETARY OF STATE

HELEN J. CUMBO
ADMINISTRATOR

SECRETARY OF STATE

Administrative Services
(225) 925-4704

Fax
(225) 925-4726
(225) 922-0435

TRANSMITTAL INFORMATION
For All Business Filings

Registered agent, officer, entity status information available via the Internet

---

Business Name (List *exactly* as it appears in documents)

Name of person filing document (evidence of filing will be mailed to this person, at address below)   Telephone number

---

Address

City   State   Zip Code

Mail or deliver the following items to the Secretary of State, at the address below:

1) This transmittal form
2) Original and one copy of the document
3) Filing fee payable to the Secretary of State

Mailing Address: P. O. Box 94125, Baton Rouge, LA * 70804-9125
Office Location: 8549 United Plaza Blvd., Baton Rouge, LA * 70809
Web Site Address: www.sos.louisiana.gov

W. Fox McKeithen
Secretary of State

ARTICLES OF ORGANIZATION
(R.S. 12:1301)

Domestic Limited Liability Company Enclose $75.00 filing fee Make remittance payable to Secretary of State *Do not send cash*	**Return to: Commercial Division** P. O. Box 94125 Baton Rouge, LA 70804-9125 Phone (225) 925-4704 Web Site: www.sos.louisiana.gov

STATE OF _____   Check one: ( ) Business   ( ) Nonprofit

PARISH/COUNTY OF _____

1. The name of this limited liability company is : _____

2. This company is formed for the purpose of: (check one)

( )   Engaging in any lawful activity for which limited liability companies may be formed.

( )   _____
                                        (use for limiting activity)

3. The duration of this limited liability company is : (may be perpetual) _____

4. Other provisions: _____

_____

_____

_____

Signatures:

_____

_____

_____

On this _____day of _____ , 200__, before me, personally appeared _____

_____ , to me known to be the person described in and who

executed the foregoing instrument, and acknowledged that he/she executed it as his/her free act and deed.

_____
Notary

W. Fox McKeithen
Secretary of State

LIMITED LIABILITY COMPANY INITIAL REPORT
(R.S. 12:1305 (E))

1. The name of this limited liability company is : _____

2. The location and municipal address, not a post office box only, of this limited liability company's
   registered office:

   _____

3. The full name and municipal address, not a post office box only, of each of this limited liability company's
   registered agent(s) is/are:

   _____

   _____

4. The names and municipal addresses, not a post office box only, of the first managers, or the members:

   _____

   _____

   _____

   To be signed by each person who signed the articles of organization:

   _____

   _____

   _____

AGENT'S AFFIDAVIT AND ACKNOWLEDGEMENT OF ACCEPTANCE

I hereby acknowledge and accept the appointment of registered agent for and on behalf of the above
named limited liability company.

Registered agent(s) signature(s):

_____

_____

Sworn to and subscribed before me, the undersigned Notary Public, on this date: _____

_____
Notary

Maine

Secretary of State
Bureau of Corporations, Elections,
and Commissions
101 State House Station
Augusta, ME 04333-0101
207-624-7736

Website:
www.state.me.us/sos/cec/corp/corp.htm

WHAT THEY SUPPLY:

State provides blank forms for Articles of Organization and Acceptance of Appointment as Registered Agent. State also provides general information on the different types of business entities, including the LLC.

WHAT MUST BE FILED:

File the typewritten or printed original Articles of Organization. If the registered agent does not sign the Articles, he or she must sign the Acceptance of Appointment as Registered Agent.

NAME REQUIREMENTS:

The name must contain the words "Limited Liability Company," "L.L.C.," or "LLC."

A Professional LLC must contain the words "Chartered," "Professional Association," or the abbreviation "P.A."

You can reserve a name by filing the application form with a $20 fee.

ARTICLES SPECIAL REQUIREMENTS:

If there are managers, a statement to that effect must be included along with the minimum and maximum number of managers. If they have been selected, their names and addresses must be included.

FILING FEES:

There is a filing fee of $125 payable to the "Secretary of State."

REPORTS:

Annual report required with $60 filing fee.

RECORDS REQUIRED:

- Names and addresses of members and managers
- Articles and all amendments
- Operating agreement and all amendments
- Past members and managers

STATUTES:

Maine Revised Statutes Title 31, Chapter 13, beginning with Section 601-762.

DOMESTIC
LIMITED LIABILITY COMPANY

STATE OF MAINE

ARTICLES OF ORGANIZATION OF
LIMITED LIABILITY COMPANY

(Mark box only if applicable)

☐ This is a professional limited liability company** formed pursuant to 13 MRSA Chapter 22-A to provide the following professional services:

_____

_____
(type of professional services)

Filing Fee $175.00

_____
Deputy Secretary of State

A True Copy When Attested By Signature

_____
Deputy Secretary of State

Pursuant to 31 MRSA §622, the undersigned executes and delivers the following Articles of Organization of Limited Liability Company:

FIRST: The name of the limited liability company is

_____.
(The name must contain one of the following: "Limited Liability Company", "L.L.C." or "LLC"; 31 MRSA §603-A.1)

SECOND: The name of its Registered Agent, an individual Maine resident or a corporation, foreign or domestic, authorized to do business or carry on activities in Maine, and the address of the registered office shall be:

_____
(name)

_____
(physical location - street (not P.O. Box), city, state and zip code)

_____
(mailing address if different from above)

THIRD: ("X" one box only)

☐   A.   The management of the company is vested in a member or members.

☐   B.   1.   The management of the company is vested in a manager or managers. The minimum number shall be _____ managers and the maximum number shall be _____ managers.

2.   If the initial managers have been selected, the name and business, residence or mailing address of each manager is:

Name   **Address**

_____   _____

_____   _____

_____   _____

☐   Names and addresses of additional managers are attached hereto as Exhibit ____, and made a part hereof.

FOURTH: Other provisions of these articles, if any, that the members determine to include are set forth in Exhibit ____ attached hereto and made a part hereof.

FORM NO. MLLC-6 (1 of 2)

Organizer(s)*

DATED _____

_____
(signature)

_____
(type or print name)

_____
(signature)

_____
(type or print name)

_____
(signature)

_____
(type or print name)

For Organizer(s) which are Entities

Name of Entity _____

By _____
(authorized signature)

_____
(type or print name and capacity)

Name of Entity _____

By _____
(authorized signature)

_____
(type or print name and capacity)

Name of Entity _____

By _____
(authorized signature)

_____
(type or print name and capacity)

Acceptance of Appointment of Registered Agent

The undersigned hereby accepts the appointment as registered agent for the above-named limited liability company.

Registered Agent

DATED _____

_____
(signature)

_____
(type or print name)

For Registered Agent which is a Corporation

Name of Corporation _____

By _____
(authorized signature)

_____
(type or print name and capacity)

Note: If the registered agent does not sign, Form MLLC-18 (31 MRSA §607.2) must accompany this document.

**Examples of professional service corporations are accountants, attorneys, chiropractors, dentists, registered nurses and veterinarians. (This is not an inclusive list – see 13 MRSA §723.7)

*Articles **MUST** be signed by:
  (1) all organizers **OR**
  (2) any duly authorized person.
The execution of this certificate constitutes an oath or affirmation under the penalties of false swearing under 17-A MRSA §453.

Please remit your payment made payable to the Maine Secretary of State.

SUBMIT COMPLETED FORMS TO: CORPORATE EXAMINING SECTION, SECRETARY OF STATE,
101 STATE HOUSE STATION, AUGUSTA, ME 04333-0101
TEL. (207) 624-7740

FORM NO. MLLC-6 (2 of 2)   Rev. 8/1/2004

Maryland

State Department of Assessments and Taxation
Corporate Charter Division
301 West Preston Street, Room 801
Baltimore, MD 21201-2395
410-767-1340
888-246-5941 (in state)

Website:
www.dat.state.md.us/sdatweb/sdatforms.html

WHAT THEY SUPPLY:

State provides instructions on how to draft your Articles of Organization and a fill-in-the-blank form of Articles.

WHAT MUST BE FILED:

Type or print your Articles, handwritten documents are not accepted. Submit the signed original for filing. If you want a certified copy, add an additional $6 plus $1 to your filing check for each additional page.

NAME REQUIREMENTS:

The company name must contain the words "Limited Liability Company," or one of the following abbreviations: "L.L.C.," "LLC," "L.C.," or "LC."

For the name availability, please check with the secretary of state at 410-767-1340. A name reservation can be made for a $7 fee.

ARTICLES SPECIAL REQUIREMENTS:

No special items are required in the Articles, but they request that the return address of the Articles be clearly noted.

FILING FEES:

There is a filing fee of $100, payable to the "State Department of Assessments & Taxation."

REPORTS:

Report must be filed every five years with filing fee of $50.

RECORDS REQUIRED:

- Names and addresses of members and managers
- Articles and all amendments
- Three years of financial records
- Three years of tax returns
- Operating agreement and all amendments

STATUTES:

Maryland Code, Corps. & Ass'ns., beginning with Section 4A-101.

ARTICLES OF ORGANIZATION

The undersigned, with the intention of creating a Maryland Limited Liability Company files the following Articles of Organization:

(1) The name of the Limited Liability Company is: _____

_____

_____.

(2) The purpose for which the Limited Liability Company is filed is as follows: _____

_____

_____.

(3) The address of the Limited Liability Company in Maryland is _____

_____.

(4) The resident agent of the Limited Liability Company in Maryland is _____

_____

whose address is _____

_____.

(5) _____   **(6)** _____
                                                        Resident Agent

_____

_____
    Signature(s) of Authorized Person(s)

Filing party's return address:

(7) _____

_____

_____

_____

Massachusetts

Secretary of the Commonwealth
Corporations Division
One Ashburton Place, 17th Floor
Boston, MA 02108
617-727-9640

Website:
www.sec.state.ma.us/cor

WHAT THEY SUPPLY:

State provides printed copies of its website. It provides instructions, how to draft your own Certificate of Organization, and general information on LLCs.

WHAT MUST BE FILED:

File the original signed copy together with a photocopy or a duplicate original. The documents must be signed either by the person forming the LLC, by any manager (if there are any), or by a trustee.

NAME REQUIREMENTS:

The company name must contain the words "Limited Liability Company," "Limited Company," or the abbreviation "L.L.C.," "L.C.," "LLC" or " LC."

It must be distinguishable from any other company name on record. You can reserve a name for thirty days by filing an application with the Division specifying the name to be reserved and the name and address of the applicant. The reservation fee is $15.

ARTICLES SPECIAL REQUIREMENTS:

If available, the Federal Employer Identification Number (FEIN) should be included on the articles. This is obtained by filing IRS form SS-4 (form 3 in appendix C). If the number is needed quickly it can be obtained over the phone (404-455-2360), but you must have form SS-4 completed and in front of you.

If there are managers, their names and residence addresses must be included. If the managers' business addresses are different from that of the LLC, their addresses must be listed.

If there is anyone other than a manager who is authorized to execute papers filed with the Corporations Division, their name and business must be included. If there are no managers, at least one member's name and business address must be listed.

FILING FEES:

There is a filing fee of $500, payable to the "Commonwealth of Massachusetts."

REPORTS:

An annual report must be filed on or before the anniversary date of the filing of its original certificate or organization. The report must contain all information required for the certificate, the annual fee is $500.

RECORDS REQUIRED:

- Names and addresses of members
- Articles and all amendments
- Three years of financial records
- Three years of tax returns
- Operating agreement and all amendments

STATUTES:

Annotated Laws of massachusetts, Title 22, Chapter 156C, Massachusetts Limited Liability Act.

Michigan

Michigan Department of Commerce
Corporation and Securities Bureau
Corporation Division
P.O. Box 30054
Lansing, MI 48909
517-241-6470

Website:
www.michigan.gov/cis

WHAT THEY SUPPLY:

The Filing Office sends you fill-in-the-blank Articles of Organization.

WHAT MUST BE FILED:

The Articles must be typed or filled in with black ink. Either form C&S 700 must be used for the Articles or it should accompany your Articles.

If you prefer the fax filing procedure, fill in the "ELF Application" form (you must provide your Visa/Mastercard number here), the cover sheet, and check the fax filing checklist (provided by the State).

NAME REQUIREMENTS:

The company name must contain the words "Limited Liability Company," or the abbreviation "L.L.C.," "LLC," "L.C.," or "LC." If you want to perform professional services, the name must contain the words "Professional Limited Liability Company," or the abbreviation "P.L.L.C." or "P.L.C."

For name availability, call 517-241-6470. You can make a reservation for a period of six months for a fee of $25. Use the Application form provided by the state.

ARTICLES SPECIAL REQUIREMENTS:

The Articles of Organization must be either on form C&S 700 (which has specific spaces for filing number, date received and return address) or a "comparable document." If you have drafted your own articles, they suggest that you attach C&S 700 as a cover sheet.

FILING FEES:

There is a $50 nonrefundable fee, payable to the "State of Michigan."

REPORTS:

Annual report required with $10 filing fee.

RECORDS REQUIRED:

- Names and addresses of members and managers
- Articles and all amendments
- Three years of financial records
- Three years of tax returns
- Operating agreement and all amendments
- Voting rights
- Terms for distributions

STATUTES:

Act 23 of the Public Acts of 1993, Michigan Limited Liability Company Act, or Michigan Compiled Laws, beginning with Section 450.4101.

BCS/CD-700 (Rev. 12/03)

| MICHIGAN DEPARTMENT OF LABOR & ECONOMIC GROWTH |
| BUREAU OF COMMERCIAL SERVICES |

Date Received	(FOR BUREAU USE ONLY)
	This document is effective on the date filed, unless a subsequent effective date within 90 days after received date is stated in the document.

Name

Address

City   State   Zip Code

EFFECTIVE DATE:

☜ **Document will be returned to the name and address you enter above.** ☞
If left blank document will be mailed to the registered office.

ARTICLES OF ORGANIZATION
For use by Domestic Limited Liability Companies

(Please read information and instructions on last page)

Pursuant to the provisions of Act 23, Public Acts of 1993, the undersigned execute the following Articles:

B

ARTICLE I

The name of the limited liability company is: _____

ARTICLE II

The purpose or purposes for which the limited liability company is formed is to engage in any activity within the purposes for which a limited liability company may be formed under the Limited Liability Company Act of Michigan.

ARTICLE III

The duration of the limited liability company if other than perpetual is:_____

ARTICLE IV

1. The street address of the location of the registered office is:

_____ , Michigan _____
(Street Address)   (City)   (ZIP Code)

2. The mailing address of the registered office if different than above:

_____ , Michigan _____
(Street Address or P.O. Box)   (City)   (ZIP Code)

3. The name of the resident agent at the registered office is: _____

ARTICLE V (Insert any desired additional provision authorized by the Act; attach additional pages if needed.)

Signed this _____ day of _____ , _____

By _____
(Signature(s) of Organizer(s))

_____
(Type or Print Name(s) of Organizer(s))

BCS/CD- 700 (Rev.12/03)

Name of person or organization remitting fees.

Preparer's Name _____   _____

Business Telephone Number _____   _____

INFORMATION AND INSTRUCTIONS

1. This form may be used to draft your Articles of Organization. A document required or permitted to be filed under the act cannot be filed unless it contains the minimum information required by the Act. The format provided contains only the minimal informaiton required to make the document fileable and may not meet your needs. This is a legal document and agency staff cannot provide legal advice.

2. Submit one original of this document. Upon filing, the document will be added to the records of the Bureau of Commercial Services. The original will be returned to your registered office address, unless you enter a different address in the box on the front of this document.

   Since this document will be maintained on electronic format, it is important that the filing be legible. Documents with poor black and white contrast, or otherwise illegible, will be rejected.

3. This document is to be used pursuant to the provisions of Act 23, P.A. of 1993, by one or more persons for the purpose of forming a domestic limited liability company. **Use form BCS/CD 701 if the limited liability company will be providing services rendered by a dentist, an osteopathic physician, a physician, a surgeon, a doctor of divinity or other clergy, or an attorney-at-law.**

4. Article I - The name of a domestic limited liability company is required to contain one of the following words or abbreviations: "Limited Liability Company", "L.L.C.", "L.C.", "LLC", or "LC".

5. Article II - Under section 203(b) of the Act, it is sufficient to state substantially, alone or with specifically enumerated purposes, that the limited liability company is formed to engage in any activity within the purposes for which a limited liability company may be formed under the Act.

6. Article V - Section 401 of the Act specifically states the business shall be managed by members unless the Articles of Organization state the business will be managed by managers. If the limited liability company is to be managed by managers instead of by members, insert a statement to that effect in Article V.

7. This document is effective on the date endorsed "Filed" by the Bureau. A later effective date, no more than 90 days after the date of delivery, may be stated as an additional article.

8. The Articles must be signed by one or more persons organizing the Limited Liability Company. State name of the organizers signing beneath their signature.

9. If more space is needed, attach additional pages. All pages should be numbered.

10. **NONREFUNDABLE FEE:** Make remittance payable to the State of Michigan. Include limited liability company name on check or money order. **$50.00**

To submit by mail:

    Michigan Department of Labor & Economic Growth
    Bureau of Commercial Services
    Corporation Division
    7150 Harris Drive
    P.O. Box 30054
    Lansing, MI 48909

To submit in person:

    2501 Woodlake Circle
    Okemos, MI
    (517) 241-6470

Fees may be paid by VISA or Mastercard when delivered in person to our office.

MICH-ELF (Michigan Electronic Filing System):

First Time Users: Call (517) 241-6470, or visit our website at http://www.michigan.gov/corporations

---

The Department of Labor & Economic Growth will not discriminate against any individual or group because of race, sex, religion, age, national origin, color, marital status, disability or political beliefs. If you need help with reading, writing, hearing, etc., under the Americans with Disabilities Act, you may make your needs known to this agency.

Minnesota

Secretary of State
Division of Corporations
180 State Office Building
100 Reverend Dr. Martin Luther King Jr. Boulevard
St. Paul, MN 55155-1299
651-296-2803
877-551-6767 (greater Minnesota)

Website:
www.sos.state.mn.us

WHAT THEY SUPPLY:

State provides one-page fill-in-the-blank Articles of Organization with instructions.

WHAT MUST BE FILED:

Type or print your articles in black ink (illegible articles will be returned). Must have original signatures.

NAME REQUIREMENTS:

The company name must include the words "Limited Liability Company" or the abbreviation "LLC" and may not include the words "Corporation" or "Incorporated."

For name availability, call 651-296-2803 between 8 a.m. and 4.30 p.m. (CT). A name may be reserved for a fee of $35.

ARTICLES SPECIAL REQUIREMENTS:

Registered agent is optional. SIC code should be provided from the following list of 19 choices:

00. Agriculture, Forestry, Fishing
10. Mining
15. Construction
20. Manufacturing—Non-Durable Goods
35. Manufacturing—Durable Goods
40. Transportation
48. Communications
49. Utilities
50. Wholesale trade
54. Retail—Non-Durable Goods
57. Retail—Durable Goods
60. Finance, Insurance, Real Estate
73. Business Services
80. Health Services
83. Social Services
86. Membership Organizations
87. Engineering and Management Services
89. Other Services
90. Other

If your LLC owns, leases, or has interest in agricultural land as described in M.S. Section 500.24 this should be stated.

FILING FEES:

There is a filing fee of $135, payable to the "Secretary of State."

REPORTS:

Biennial report required.

RECORDS REQUIRED:

- Names and addresses of members and managers
- Articles and all amendments
- Three years of financial records
- Three years of tax returns
- Operating agreement and all amendments
- Voting rights
- Terms for distributions

STATUTES:

Chapter 322 B Minnesota Statutes.

MINNESOTA SECRETARY OF STATE

ARTICLES OF ORGANIZATION FOR A LIMITED LIABILITY COMPANY

MINNESOTA STATUTES CHAPTER 322B

PLEASE TYPE OR PRINT IN BLACK INK.

Before Completing this Form Please Read the Instructions on the Back.   FILING FEE $135.00

1. Name of Company:_____

2. Registered Office Address:**(P.O. Box is Unacceptable)**

_____ MN _____
Complete Street Address or Rural Route and Rural Route Box Number   City   State   ZIP Code

3. Name of Registered Agent (optional): _____

4. Business Mailing Address: (if different from registered office address)

_____
Address   City   State   ZIP Code

5. Desired Duration of LLC: (in years) _____(If you do not complete this item, a perpetual duration is assumed by law.)

6. Does this LLC own, lease or have any interest in agricultural land or land capable of being farmed?
     (Check One)   Yes _____   No _____

7. Name and Address of Organizer(s):

Name (print)	Complete Address Street City State Zip	Original Signature (required)

8. Name and Telephone Number of Contact Person for this LLC:

Name _____

Phone (_____)_____

bus88   Rev. 3-03

Mississippi

Secretary of State
Business Services Division
P.O. Box 136
Jackson, MS 39205
601-359-1633
800-256-3494

Website:
www.sos.state.ms.us/busserv/corp/corporations.asp

WHAT THEY SUPPLY:

State provides computer-readable fill-in-the-blank forms with precise instructions on how to meet the special requirements.

WHAT MUST BE FILED:

For computer legibility make sure you fill in the forms exactly as described in the instructions. File the original copy signed by the person forming the limited liability company. Enclose the filing fee.

NAME REQUIREMENTS:

The company name must contain the words "Limited Liability Company," or the abbreviation "LLC" or "L.L.C." A name reservation is possible for a fee of $25.

ARTICLES SPECIAL REQUIREMENTS:

The Mississippi form is bar coded and meant to be machine-readable. Using their form will speed up your filing, but it is not required.

You need to provide the Federal Employer Identification Number (F.E.I.N.), which must be obtained prior to filing. This is obtained by filing IRS form SS-4 (form 3 in appendix C). If the number is needed quickly it can be obtained over the phone (404-455-2360), but you must have form SS-4 completed and in front of you.

The name of the company is limited to 120 characters on the bar-coded form, and some other information is limited in the number of characters allowed.

FILING FEES:

There is a filing fee of $50, payable to the "Secretary of State."

REPORTS:

No annual fee.

RECORDS REQUIRED:

- Names and addresses of members and managers
- Articles and all amendments
- Operating agreement and all amendments

STATUTES:

Mississippi Code beginning with Section 79-29-101.

F0100 - Page 1 of 2

OFFICE OF THE MISSISSIPPI SECRETARY OF STATE
P.O. BOX 136, JACKSON, MS 39205-0136   (601) 359-1333
Certificate of Formation

The undersigned, pursuant to Senate Bill No. 2395, Chapter 402, Laws of 1994, hereby executes the following document and sets forth:

1. Name of the Limited Liability Company

2. The future effective date is
   (Complete if applicable)

3. Federal Tax ID

4. Name and Street Address of the Registered Agent and Registered Office is

Name

Physical
Address

P.O. Box

City, State, ZIP5, ZIP4

5. If the Limited Liability Company is to have a specific date of dissolution, the latest date upon which the Limited Liability Company is to dissolve

6. Is full or partial management of the Limited Liability Company vested in a manager or managers? (Mark appropriate box)

Yes   No

7. Other matters the managers or members elect to include

Rev. 01/96

OFFICE OF THE MISSISSIPPI SECRETARY OF STATE
P.O. BOX 136, JACKSON, MS 39205-0136   (601) 359-1333
Certificate of Formation

By: Signature

(Please keep writing within blocks)

Printed Name   Title

Street and Mailing Address

Physical Address

P.O. Box

City, State, ZIP5, ZIP4   -

By: Signature

(Please keep writing within blocks)

Printed Name   Title

Street and Mailing Address

Physical Address

P.O. Box

City, State, ZIP5, ZIP4   -

LLC ARTICLES OF ORGANIZATION (Domestic & foreign -T.11,Ch.21)

Vermont Secretary of State, 81 River Street, Montpelier, VT 05609-1104.

Name of LLC: _____
(Name must contain the words Limited Liability Company, Limited Company, LLC, LC)

Organized under the laws of the state (or country) of: _____
Foreign LLC must attach a good standing cert, dated no earlier than 30 days prior to filing, from its State of origin.

Principal office: _____
_____

Registered agent: _____
Agent's street & po box: _____
  VERMONT _____

The fiscal year ends the month of: _____ (DEC will be designated as the month your year ends unless you state differently.) Each company under this title is required to file an *annual report* within 2 1/2 months of the close of its fiscal year. Failure to file may result in termination of the its authority. A pre-printed form will be mailed to your agent when the report is due.

Is this a *term* LLC? ☐ Yes ☐ No If Yes, state duration of its term: _____
An LLC is an At-Will Company unless it is designated in its articles as a Term Co)

This is a MANAGER-MANAGED company? ☐ Yes ☐ No If yes list name & address below
_____
_____
_____

Are members personally liable for debts & obligations under T.11,§3043(b)? ☐ Yes ☐ No

Printed Name _____   Signature _____   date: _____
Organizers address: _____
_____ Fees: VT domestic = $ 75.00 Foreign
(non-Vt) = $100.00 Print & file in duplicate. If a delayed effective date is not specified | date _____ | (no later than 90 days after filing), it is effective the date it is approved.
Give your email add. or phone # so we can contact you with questions: _____ (rev 7/01)

Virginia

Clerk of the State Corporation Commission
P.O. Box 1197
Richmond, VA 23218
804-371-9733

Website:
www.state.va.us/scc/division/clk

WHAT THEY SUPPLY:

State provides fill-in-the-blank Articles of Organization with simple instructions and a fee schedule.

WHAT MUST BE FILED:

The Articles must be printed or typewritten in black ink. Complete and file the original form and enclose the filing fee.

NAME REQUIREMENTS:

The name must contain the words "Limited Company" or "Limited Liability Company" or the abbreviations "L.C.," "LC," "L.L.C.," or "LLC."

A name reservation can be made for 120 days by filing an application (form LLC-1013) with a $10 fee.

ARTICLES SPECIAL REQUIREMENTS:

The registered agent must be an individual who is a Virginia resident and either a member or an officer, director or partner of a member of the LLC, or a Virginia State Bar member, or an organization registered under Va. Code Section 54.1-3902 (an attorney's PC, PLLC, or PRLLP) and this must be stated in the Articles.

The city or county of the registered agent must be included and also the post office address of the office where the records will be kept.

The Articles can be executed by any person.

FILING FEES:

There is a filing fee of $100, payable to the "State Corporation Commission." Pay by check or similar payment method, no cash accepted. A certified copy is $6.

REPORTS:

Annual report required with $50 filing fee. The fee is due each year before September 1, beginning the year after the calendar year in which your company was organized.

RECORDS REQUIRED:

- Names and addresses of members and managers
- Articles and all amendments
- Three years of financial records
- Three years of tax returns
- Three years operating agreements

STATUTES:

Title 13.1 of the Code of Virginia.

LLC-1011
(07/04)

COMMONWEALTH OF VIRGINIA
STATE CORPORATION COMMISSION

ARTICLES OF ORGANIZATION OF A
DOMESTIC LIMITED LIABILITY COMPANY

Pursuant to Chapter 12 of Title 13.1 of the Code of Virginia the undersigned states as follows:

1. The name of the limited liability company is

_____.

(The name must contain the words "limited company" or "limited liability company" or the abbreviation "L.C.", "LC", "L.L.C." or "LLC")

2. A. The name of the limited liability company's initial registered agent is

_____

B. The registered agent is **(mark appropriate box):**

(1) an <u>INDIVIDUAL</u> who is a resident of Virginia **and**
   [ ] a member or manager of the limited liability company.
   [ ] a member or manager of a limited liability company that is a member or manager of the limited
       liability company.
   [ ] an officer or director of a corporation that is a member or manager of the limited liability company.
   [ ] a general partner of a general or limited partnership that is a member or manager of the limited
       liability company.
   [ ] a trustee of a trust that is a member or manager of the limited liability company.
   [ ] a member of the Virginia State Bar.
                                        OR
(2) [ ] a domestic or foreign stock or nonstock corporation, limited liability company or registered limited
       liability partnership authorized to transact business in Virginia.

3. The limited liability company's initial registered office address, including the street and number, if any,
   which is identical to the business office of the initial registered agent, is

   _____
   (number/street)

   _____ VA _____,
   (city or town)   (zip)

   which is located in the [ ] city **or** [ ] county of _____.

4. The limited liability company's principal office address, including the street and number, if any, is

   _____.
   (number/street)

   _____   _____   _____.
   (city or town)   (state)   (zip)

5. Organizer:

   _____   _____
   (signature)   (date)

   _____   _____
   (printed name)   (telephone number (optional))

SEE INSTRUCTIONS ON THE REVERSE

Washington

Secretary of State
Corporations Division
P.O. Box 40234
Olympia, WA 98504-0234
360-753-7115

Website:
www.secstate.wa.gov/corps

WHAT THEY SUPPLY:

State provides single copy of fill-in-the-blank Certificate of Formation form.

WHAT MUST BE FILED:

Type or print the document in black ink. Submit original and one copy. If expedited service is desired write "expedited" in bold letters on outside of envelope and include the additional fee.

NAME REQUIREMENTS:

Your company name must contain the words "Limited Liability Company," "Limited Liability Co.," or the abbreviation "L.L.C." or "LLC."

For a $30 fee, you can reserve an LLC name for a period of 180 days.

ARTICLES SPECIAL REQUIREMENTS:

There are no unusual requirements.

FILING FEES:

There is a filing fee of $175, payable to the "Secretary of State." Expedited service of twenty-four hour turn around is available for an additional $20.

REPORTS:

Your first annual report has to be filed within 120 days of filing your Certificate of Formation. The fee is $10. After that your annual report is due on the date determined by the secretary of state. The report form is provided by the secretary of state.

RECORDS REQUIRED:

- Names and addresses of members and managers
- Articles and all amendments
- Three years of financial records
- Three years of tax returns
- Operating agreement and amendments
- Past members and managers
- Contributions

STATUTES:

Chapter 25.15 Revised Code of Washington.

West Virginia

Secretary of State
Building 1, Suite 157-K
1900 Kanawha Boulevard East
Charleston, WV 25305-0770
304-558-8000

Website:
www.wvsos.com/business/main.htm

WHAT THEY SUPPLY:

State provides a booklet, "Applications and Instructions for Business Start-Up," instructions for filing Articles of Organization, and two copies of fill-in-the-blank Articles of Organization.

WHAT MUST BE FILED:

Two original copies of the Articles of Organization must be filed.

NAME REQUIREMENTS:

Your company name must contain the words "Limited Liability Company," "Limited Company," or the abbreviations "LLC," L.L.C.," "LC," or "L.C." "Limited" and "company" may not be abbreviated as "Ltd." and "Co." It may not use the words "Corporation," "Incorporated," "Limited Partnership," or the abbreviations "Corp.," or "Inc."

Professional companies must use "Professional Limited Liability Company," "Professional L.L.C.," "Professional LLC," "P.L.L.C.," or "PLLC."

Name may be reserved for 120 days for $15.

ARTICLES SPECIAL REQUIREMENTS:

It is possible to designate members to be liable for company debts. This is neither required nor recommended, as it defeats the purpose of the limited liability company. However, the statement needs to be included in your Articles.

FILING FEES:

There is a filing fee of $100, payable to the "Secretary of State." Add $15 for each certified copy of Articles requested.

REPORTS:

The annual report is due each year between January 1 and April 1. The fee is $25.

RECORDS REQUIRED:

- No requirement

STATUTES:

Chapter 31B, beginning with Section 1-101, Uniform Limited Liability Company Act.

Betty Ireland
Secretary of State
State Capitol Building
1900 Kanawha Blvd. East
Charleston, WV 25305-0770

Penney Barker, Manager
Corporations Division
Tel: (304) 558-8000
Fax: (304) 558-5758
Hours: 8:30 a.m. - 5:00 p.m. ET

WEST VIRGINIA
ARTICLES OF ORGANIZATION
OF LIMITED LIABILITY COMPANY

Control #_ _ _ _ _ _

We, acting as organizers according to West Virginia Code §31B-2-202, adopt the following Articles of Organization for a West Virginia Limited Liability Company:

1. The **name** of the **West Virginia limited liability company** shall be: [The name must contain one of the required terms such as "limited liability company" or abbreviations such as "LLC" or "PLLC"--see instructions for list of acceptable terms.]

_____

_____

2. The company will be an: ☐ LLC ☐ professional LLC for the profession of _____

3. The **address** of the initial **designated office** of the company in WV, if any, will be:
[need not be a place of the company's business]

Street: _____

City/State/Zip: _____ WV _____

4. The mailing address of the **principal office,** if different, will be:

Street/Box: _____

City/State/Zip: _____

5. The name and address of the **agent for service of process**, if any, is:

Name: _____

Street: _____

City/State/Zip: _____

The mailing address of the above agent of process, if different, is:

Street/Box: _____

City/State/Zip: _____

6. The name and address of each organizer:

<u>Name</u>	<u>No. & Street</u>	<u>City, State, Zip</u>
_____	_____	_____
_____	_____	_____
_____	_____	_____

7. The company will be:

☐ an at-will company, for an indefinite period.

☐ a term company, for the term of ____ years.

WEST VIRGINIA ARTICLES OF ORGANIZATION OF LIMITED LIABILITY COMPANY   Page 2

8. The Company will be:

☐ **member-managed.** [List the name and address of each member with signature authority, attach an extra sheet if needed]

OR ☐ **manager-managed,** [List the name and address of each manager with signature authority, attach an extra sheet if needed.]

Name	Address	City, State, Zip

9. All or specified members of a limited liability company are liable in their capacity as members for all or specified debts, obligations or liabilities of the company.

☐ NO -- All debts, obligations and liabilities are those of the company.

☐ YES -- Those persons who are liable in their capacity as members for all debts, obligations or liability of the company have consented to this in writing.

10. The **purposes** for which this limited liability company is formed are as follows:
(Describe the type(s) of business activity which will be conducted, for example, "real estate," "construction of residential and commercial buildings," "commercial printing," "professional practice of architecture.")

11. Other provisions which may be set forth in the operating agreement or matters not inconsistent with law:
[See instructions for further information; use extra pages if necessary.]

12. The number of pages attached and included in these Articles is _____.

13. The requested effective date is: ☐ the date & time of filing
[Requested date may not be earlier than filing nor later than 90 days after filing.]

☐ the following date _____ and time_____

14. **Contact and Signature Information:**

a. Contact person to reach in case there is a problem with filing: _____

Phone #_____

Business email address, if any: _____

b. Signature of : (manager of a manager-manged company, member of a member-managed company, person organizing the company, if the company has not been formed or attorney-in-fact for any of the above.

_____   _____   _____
Name [print or type]   Title/Capacity   Signature

Betty Ireland
Secretary of State
State Capitol Building
1900 Kanawha Blvd. East
Charleston, WV 25305-0770

Penney Barker, Manager
CORPORATIONS DIVISION
Tel: (304) 558-8000
Fax: (304) 558-5758
Hours: 8:30 a.m. - 5:00 p.m. ET

INSTRUCTIONS FOR FILING
ARTICLES OF ORGANIZATION
FOR A WEST VIRGINIA L.L.C. or P.L.L.C.

BEFORE you fill out the application: The company name you select will be approved **only** if it is available-- that is, if the name is not the same as and is distinguishable from any other name which has been reserved or filed. If you prepare LLC papers without applying for and receiving a name reservation, you do so at your own risk. A telephone check on availability of a name is not a guarantee.

You may apply for a name reservation in writing, accompanied by a $15 fee payable to the Secretary of State, mailed to the address shown above. Once approved, you are guaranteed exclusive use of the name for 120 days, enough time to prepare and submit the articles.

If you plan to do business under any name, other than the name on your certificate of organization, you must register that trade name with the Secretary of State. Failure to do so could result in a fine or imprisonment.

FILLING OUT THE APPLICATION:

Section 1. Enter the exact **name** of the company, and be sure to include one of the required terms: "limited liability company," "limited company," or the abbreviations "L.L.C.", "LLC", "L.C." or "LC". "Limited" may be abbreviated a "Ltd." and "Company" may be abbreviated as "Co." [WV Code §31B-1-105] Professional companies must use "professional limited liability company," "professional L.L.C.", "professional LLC", "P.L.L.C." or "PLLC". [WV Code §31B-13-1303]

Section 2. Check the first box unless your company qualifies as a professional LLC. A professional LLC may be organized only by one or more persons licensed or otherwise legally authorized to provide the same or compatible professional services or to practice together within the state. No person may be a member of the PLLC who is not licensed or otherwise legally authorized to render the profession service for which the PLLC was organized. Only the following professions listed below under the specified articles of Chapter 30 of West Virginia Code may form a PLLC. If you are a member of another profession, please contact your licensing board before attempting to establish your business as a regular LLC.

Attorneys-at-law	[Article 2]	Physicians & podiatrists	[Article 3]
Dentists	[Article 4]	Optometrists	[Article 8]
Accountants	[Article 9]	Veterinarians	[Article 10]
Architects	[Article 12]	Engineers	[Article 13]
Osteopathic physicians and surgeons	[Article 14]	Chiropractors	[Article 16]
		Psychologists	[Article 30]
		Land Surveyors	[Article 13a]

Important! The secretary of state cannot complete your filing until confirmation is received from the licensing board that the licenses of your members are current and in effect. A PLLC is required to carry at all times at $1 million of professional liability insurance. [See W. Va. Code §31B-13-1305]

Section 3. The designated office need not be the principal place of business. You may change the designated office by filing with the secretary of state a statement of change giving the company name, old address and new address for the designated office (fee $15).

Section 4. Please list the mailing address of your principal office.

Section 5. You may wish to maintain an **"agent of process"** in West Virginia who can receive service of a summons or complaint. The agent may be an individual resident of the state, a domestic corporation, another limited liability company or a foreign corporation or foreign company authorized to do business in this state. Your may change your agent by filing with the secretary of state a statement of change giving both the current and new agent's name and address, as well as the agent's written consent to act as agent (fee $15).

Section 6. One or more persons may organize a limited liability company. The name and address of each organizer having authority to execute instruments on behalf of the limited liability company is required.

Section 7. An **at-will company** will continue to exist until voluntarily terminated or administratively dissolved. A **term company** is one in which its members have agreed to remain members until the expiration of a term specified in the articles. If neither box is marked or the length of the term not specified, the company will be established as an at-will company.

Section 8. For a *member-managed company*, the authority to transact business and execute instruments is in the hands of the members, and any member may act to carry on the ordinary course of company's business as an agent of the company. For a *manager-managed company*, a manager, who may or may not be a member, is an agent of the company for the purpose of its business. See WV Code §31B for more information about the authority of members & managers. You need to list any members or managers with signature authority.

Section 9. Do not check yes to this question <u>unless</u> and <u>until</u> you have in hand the written consent of those members who are liable for all debts, obligations and liabilities of the company agreeing to the adoption of or to be bound by this provision in the operating agreement. The liabilities may not be assigned on the belief that members will consent.

Section 10. The State Tax Department requests that you describe the **purposes** of the limited liability company clearly to insure you receive all the necessary information about registering with the required state agencies. **Please note that filing articles of organization alone does not qualify you to do business in West Virginia. You must obtain a business license from the Department of Tax and Revenue, and you may be required to meet other licensing requirements to do the type of business you intend.** Attach an extra page if needed.

Section 11. The articles may include provisions permitted to be set forth in an operating agreement [but may not vary the non-waivable provisions of W. Va. Code §31B-1-103(b)] and other matters not inconsistent with law. If any provision of the operating agreement is inconsistent with the articles of organization, the articles control as to persons other than managers, members and their transferees who reasonably rely on the articles to their detriment.

Section 12. Give the number of attached pages to insure your complete filing is recorded.

Section 13. You may accept the date of filing as your effective date, or assign a <u>future</u> date and time when the company will be activated. If the date you give is more than 90 days after the filing date, the active date will be the 90th day after filing. If you do not specify a time, the filing is effective at the close of business on that date.

Section 14. The articles must be signed by a person in one of the four categories listed in section 14. If a person acts as attorney-in-fact for the company in signing this or other documents, the power of attorney need not be filed with the secretary of state but must be kept by the company.

NOTICE: W. Va. Code §31B-2-211 requires every limited liability company to file an annual report and pay an annual attorney-in-fact fee between January 1 and April 1 of <u>each</u> year following the calendar year in which you begin business in WV.

Fee for filing Articles of Organization

Fee for filing Articles of Organization	$100
Attorney-in-fact fee (from chart)	+
Add $15 for each certified copy of articles requested	+
Amount enclosed, payable to Secretary of State	_____

Fee schedule for Att-in-fact
These fees are prorated based on the month in which application will be received

Jan	100%	$25	May	80%	$20	Sept.	40%	$10
Feb	100%	$25	June	70%	$17.50	Oct.	30%	$7.50
Mar	100%	$25	July	60%	$15	Nov.	20%	$5
Apr	90%	$22.50	Aug	50%	$12.50	Dec.	10%	$2.50

Wisconsin

Department of Financial Institutions
Division of Corporate and Consumer Services
P.O. Box 7846
Madison, WI 53707-7846
608-261-7577

Website:
www.wisconsin.gov or
www.wdfi.org/corporations

WHAT THEY SUPPLY:

State provides two copies of fill-in-the-blank Articles of Organization with instruction sheet and fee schedule.

WHAT MUST BE FILED:

Original and one copy must be filed.

For expedited service (filing procedure will be complete the next business day), mark your documents "For Expedited Service" and provide an extra $25 for each item. Indicate on the back side of your Articles where you would like the acknowledgement copy of the filed document sent.

Use the above address for mail. For courier delivery use 345 West Washington Avenue, 3rd Floor, Madison, WI 53703.

NAME REQUIREMENTS:

Your company name must contain the words "Limited Liability Company" or "Limited Liability Co." or must end with the abbreviations "L.L.C." or "LLC."

For name availability, call the filing office prior to filing. A name can be reserved either by calling 608-261-9555 or by a written application. The application must include the name and address of the applicant and the name proposed to be reserved. If the name is available, it will be reserved for 120 days. The reservation fee is $15 by mail or $30 by phone. The name can be renewed for an additional 120 days for the same fees.

If your first choice is not available, you can provide a second choice name on the reverse side of your Articles.

ARTICLES SPECIAL REQUIREMENTS:

The Articles for a Wisconsin LLC can *only* contain items of information such as:

- The name
- The street address of the initial registered office
- The name of the initial registered agent at the above address
- Whether management is vested in the members or manager(s)
- The name, address, and signature of each organizer
- A statement that the company is organized under Wisconsin statutes, Chapter 183
- The name of the person who drafted the articles

Other terms between members can be included in the operating agreement.

FILING FEES:

There is a $170 filing fee. For expedited service, add an additional $25 for each item. If you file your Articles electronically via the Internet (www.wdfi.org, click on "Create an LLC"), the filing fee is $130, including the charge for expedited processing. If you file via Internet the fee is only payable by Visa or Mastercard.

REPORTS:

No annual reporting fee.

RECORDS REQUIRED:

- Names and addresses of members and managers
- Articles and all amendments
- Three years of financial records
- Three years of tax returns
- Operating agreement and amendments
- Must be kept in principal office

STATUTES:

Chapter 183 of the Wisconsin Statutes.

Sec. 183.0202
Wis. Stats.

State of Wisconsin
Department of Financial Institutions
Division of Corporate and Consumer Services

ARTICLES OF ORGANIZATION - LIMITED LIABILITY COMPANY

Executed by the undersigned for the purpose of forming a Wisconsin limited liability company under Ch. 183 of the Wisconsin Statutes:

Article 1. Name of the limited liability company:

_____

Article 2. The limited liability company is organized under Ch. 183 of the Wisconsin Statutes.

Article 3. Name of the initial registered agent: _____

Article 4. Street address of the initial registered office: _____
(*The complete address, including street and number, if
assigned, and ZIP code. P O Box address may be*   _____
included as part of the address, but is insufficient alone.)

_____

Article 5. Management of the limited liability company shall be vested in:
        (Select and check (**X**) the one appropriate choice below)

    ☐ a manager or managers

OR

    ☐ its members

Article 6. **Name** and **complete address** of each organizer:

_____   _____

        Organizer's signature   Organizer's signature

This document was drafted by _____
                      (Name the individual who drafted the document)

➤ OPTIONAL – Second choice company name if first choice is not available:

FILING FEE - $170.00 See instructions, suggestions, and procedures on following pages.
(Note: Electronic edition of this form is "Quickstart LLC," available at www.wdfi.org at a lower fee.)
DFI/CORP/**502**(R04/22/03) Use of this form is voluntary.   1 of 2

ARTICLES OF ORGANIZATION - Limited Liability Company

Γ

L

➤ Your **name, return address** and **phone number** during the day (   ) _____ - _____

INSTRUCTIONS (Ref. sec. 183.0202 Wis. Stats. for document content)

Submit one original and one exact copy to Department of Financial Institutions, P O Box 7846, Madison WI, 53707-7846, together with the appropriate **FILING FEE of $170**. Filing fee is **non-refundable**. (If sent by Express or Priority U.S. mail, address to 345 W. Washington Ave., 3rd Floor, Madison WI, 53703). Sign the document manually or otherwise as allowed under sec. 183.0107(2), Wis. Stats. **NOTICE**: This form may be used to accomplish a filing required or permitted by statute to be made with the department. Information requested may be used for secondary purposes. If you have any questions, please contact the Division of Corporate & Consumer Services at 608-261-7577. Hearing-impaired may call 608-266-8818 for TTY. This document can be made available in alternate formats upon request to qualifying individuals with disabilities.

Article 1. The name must contain the words "limited liability company" or "limited liability co." or end with the abbreviation "L.L.C." or "LLC". If you wish to provide a second choice name that you would accept if your first choice is not available, enter it in the "Optional" area on page 1.

Article 2. This statement is required by sec. 183.0202(1).

Articles 3 & 4. The company must have a registered agent located at a registered office in Wisconsin. The address of the registered office is to describe the physical location where the registered agent maintains their business office. Provide the street number and name, city and ZIP code in Wisconsin. P O Box addresses may be included as part of the address, but are insufficient alone. The company may not name itself as its own registered agent.

Article 5. Indicate whether management of the company will be vested in a manager or managers, or in its members. Select only one choice. (Ref. sec. 183.0401, Wis. Stats.)

Article 6. Print or typewrite the name and complete address of each organizer. At least one organizer is required to sign the document, although all organizers may sign.

If the document is executed in Wisconsin, sec. 182.01(3), Wis. Stats., provides that it shall not be filed unless the name of the drafter (either an individual or a governmental agency) is printed in a legible manner. If the document is not executed in Wisconsin, enter that remark.

This document may declare a delayed effective date. To do so, enter a remark: "This document has a delayed effective date of   (enter the future date)   ."   The delayed effective date may not before, or more than 90 days after, the document is received by the Department of Financial Institutions for filing.

NOTE: The articles of organization may contain **only** that information required under items 1 through 6. The company may create a separate operating agreement that includes additional information.

DFI/CORP/**502**(R04/22/03)

Wyoming

Corporations Division
Secretary of State
The Capital Building
Room 110
200 West 24ᵗʰ Street
Cheyenne, WY 82002-0020
307-777-7311

Website:
http://soswy.state.wy.us/corporat/corporat.htm

WHAT THEY SUPPLY:

State provides fill-in-the-blank form of Articles of Organization and "Consent to Appointment by Registered Agent" with instructions how to complete these forms.

WHAT MUST BE FILED:

An original and one exact copy must be filed along with a written consent to appointment by the registered agent.

NAME REQUIREMENTS:

The company name must contain the words "Limited Liability Company" or "Limited Company," or the abbreviation "L.L.C.," "LLC," "L.C.," or "LC." It can also contain the combination "Ltd Liability Co." or "Limited Liability Co." or "Ltd. Liability Company."

A name can be reserved for a fee of $50 for a 120 day period.

ARTICLES SPECIAL REQUIREMENTS:

The total of cash, a description, the agreed value of property other than cash contributed to the company, and any additional capital agreed to be contributed must be included in the Articles.

If there is a right to admit new members the terms of admission must be stated.

If the members have a right to continue the business after the termination of a member this must be stated.

The Articles must accompany a written consent by the registered agent to appointment as agent.

FILING FEES:

The filing fee is $100.

REPORTS:

The annual report is due on the first day of the month of registration. The fee is $50 or two tenths of one million on the dollar ($.0002), whichever is greater based on the company's assets located and employed in the state of Wyoming.

RECORDS REQUIRED:

- Written operating agreement
- Minutes of meetings

STATUTES:

Wyoming Statute beginning with 17-15-101.

ARTICLES OF ORGANIZATION
FOR A DOMESTIC LIMITED LIABILITY COMPANY

Wyoming Secretary of State
The Capitol Building, Room 110
200 W. 24th Street
Cheyenne, WY 82002-0020

Phone (307) 777-7311/7312
Fax (307) 777-5339
E-mail: corporations@state.wy.us

1.   The name of the limited liability company is: _____
     _____

2.   The period of its duration is: _____
     (This is the length of time the LLC intends to exist. It may be listed as "perpetual," a certain number of years such as "30 years," or may be listed as a specific date such as "Dec. 31, 2055")

3.   The purpose for which the limited liability company is organized is: _____
     _____
     _____
     _____

4.   The name and address of its registered agent is: _____
     _____
     _____
     (The registered agent may be an individual resident in this state or a domestic or foreign corporation authorized to transact business in this state, having a business office identical with such registered office. Do not use a Post Office Box or Mail Drop Box)

5.   The mailing address where correspondence and annual report forms can be sent:
     _____
     _____

6.   The total amount of cash and a description and agreed value of property other than cash contributed is: _____
     _____
     _____
     _____

7.   The total additional contributions, if any, agreed to be made by all members and the times at which or events upon the happening of which they shall be made are: _____
     _____
     _____
     _____

8.   The right, if given, of the members to admit additional members, and the terms and conditions of the admission are: _____
     _____
     _____
     _____

9.   The right, if given, of the remaining members of the limited liability company to continue the business on the death, resignation, expulsion, bankruptcy or dissolution of a member or occurrence of any other event which terminates the continued membership of a member of the limited liability company:

_____

_____

_____

_____

10. **Complete either item #1 or item #2**

1) The limited liability company is to be managed by a manager or managers. The names and addresses of the managers who are to serve as managers until the first annual meeting of the members or until their successors are elected and qualify are: _____

_____

_____

_____

_____

2) The management of the limited liability company is reserved to the members. The names and addresses of the members are: _____

_____

_____

_____

_____

Date: _____   Signed: _____

_____

_____

_____

Filing Fee: $100.00

Instructions:

1.   The name must include the words "Limited Liability Company," or its abbreviations "LLC" or "L.L.C.," "Limited Company," or its abbreviations "LC" or "L.C.," "Ltd. Liability Company," "Ltd. Liability Co." or "Limited Liability Co.".

2.   Articles must be accompanied by a written consent to appointment executed by the registered agent.

3.   Make check payable to Secretary of State.

llcda - Revised: 12/2003

CONSENT TO APPOINTMENT
BY REGISTERED AGENT

Wyoming Secretary of State   Phone (307) 777-7311/7312
The Capitol Building, Room 110   Fax (307) 777-5339
200 W. 24th Street   E-mail: corporations@state.wy.us
Cheyenne, WY 82002-0020

I, _____ , voluntarily consent to serve as the

registered agent for _____

on the date shown below.

The registered agent certifies that he is: (check one)

☐   *(a)*   *An individual who resides in this state and whose business office is identical with the registered office;*

☐   *(b)*   *A domestic corporation or not-for-profit domestic corporation whose business office is identical with the registered office; or*

☐   *(c)*   *A foreign corporation or not-for-profit foreign corporation authorized to transact business in this state whose business office is identical with the registered office.*

Dated this _____ day of _____, _____.

_____
Signature of Registered Agent

Revised: 12/2003

Appendix B:
Sample, Filled-In Forms

TRANSMITTAL LETTER

To: Secretary of State
         Corporation Division
         State Capitol, Rm. 100
         Libertyville, FL 33757

Re: Williams and Johnson, L.L.C

Enclosed is an original and ___1___ copies of Articles of Organization for the above-referenced LLC along with a check for $___125____ as follows:

         $__125___ for filing fee
         $___---___ for _____

Please send acknowledgement of receipt and/or date-stamped copy to:

                        Bill Williams
                        Williams and Johnson, L.L.C.
                        123 Liberty Street
                        Libertyville, FL 33757

ARTICLES OF ORGANIZATION FOR A LIMITED LIABILITY COMPANY

ARTICLE I - Name:

The name of the Limited Liability Company is:

Williams and Johnson, L.L.C

ARTICLE II - Purpose:

The purpose for which this limited liability company is organized is:

to engage in any and all lawful acts for which an L.L.C. may be formed.

ARTICLE III - Duration:

The period of duration for the Limited Liability Company shall be: perpetual

ARTICLE IV - Registered (or Statutory) Agent and Address:

The name and address of the initial registered (statutory) agent is:

Bill Willliams, 123 Liberty Street, Libertyville, FL 33757

ARTICLE V - Management:
(Check the appropriate box and complete the statement)

❑ The Limited Liability Company is to be managed by a manager or managers and the name(s) and address(es) of such manager(s) who is/are to serve as manager(s) is/are:

☒ The Limited Liability Company is to be managed by the members and the name(s) and address(es) of the managing members is/are:

Bill Willliams, 123 Liberty Street, Libertyville, FL 33757
John Johnson, 605 Galt Street, Libertyville, FL 33757

ARTICLE VI - Principal Place of Business

The initial principal place of business of the Limited Liability Company is:

123 Liberty Street, Libertyville, FL 33757

ARTICLE VII - Effective Date

The effective date of these articles is ☒ upon filing   ❑ on _____

ARTICLE VIII - Nonliability

The members and managers, if any, shall not be liable for any debts, obligations, or liabilities of the limited liability company.

ARTICLE IX - Miscellaneous

New members can be admitted to the company with full rights of membership upon the unanimous consent of the existing members.

IN WITNESS WHEREOF, the undersigned members executed these Articles of Organization this __22__ day of
__March__, __2006__.

Bill Williams
_____
Member: Bill Williams   Address:
123 Liberty Street, Libertyville, FL 33757

John Johnson
_____
Member: John Johnson   Address:
605 Galt Street, Libertyville, FL 33757

_____
Member: Address:

_____
Member: Address:

Acceptance of Registered (Statutory) Agent

Having been named as registered agent and to accept service of process for the above stated limited liability company at the place designated in this certificate, I hereby accept the appointment as registered agent and agree to act in this capacity. I further agree to comply with the provisions of all statutes relating to the proper and complete performance of my duties, and am familiar with and accept the obligations of my position as registered agent.

Bill Williams
_____
Agent: Bill Williams

Form **SS-4**

(Rev. December 2001)

Department of the Treasury
Internal Revenue Service

Application for Employer Identification Number

(For use by employers, corporations, partnerships, trusts, estates, churches,
government agencies, Indian tribal entities, certain individuals, and others.)

· See separate instructions for each line.   · Keep a copy for your records.

EIN

OMB No. 1545-0003

Type or print clearly.

1 Legal name of entity (or individual) for whom the EIN is being requested	
Williams and Johnson, L.L.C.	

2 Trade name of business (if different from name on line 1)	**3** Executor, trustee, "care of" name

4a Mailing address (room, apt., suite no. and street, or P.O. box)	**5a** Street address (if different) (Do not enter a P.O. box.)
123 Liberty Street	
4b City, state, and ZIP code	**5b** City, state, and ZIP code
Libertyville, FL 33757	

6 County and state where principal business is located
Liberty County, FL

7a Name of principal officer, general partner, grantor, owner, or trustor	**7b** SSN, ITIN, or EIN
Bill Williams	123-45-6789

8a Type of entity (check only one box)

- [ ] Sole proprietor (SSN) _____
- [ ] Partnership
- [ ] Corporation (enter form number to be filed) · _____
- [ ] Personal service corp.
- [ ] Church or church-controlled organization
- [ ] Other nonprofit organization (specify) · _____
- [X] Other (specify) · LLC

- [ ] Estate (SSN of decedent) _____
- [ ] Plan administrator (SSN) _____
- [ ] Trust (SSN of grantor) _____
- [ ] National Guard   [ ] State/local government
- [ ] Farmers' cooperative   [ ] Federal government/military
- [ ] REMIC   [ ] Indian tribal governments/enterprises
- Group Exemption Number (GEN) · _____

8b If a corporation, name the state or foreign country (if applicable) where incorporated

State	Foreign country

9 Reason for applying (check only one box)

- [X] Started new business (specify type) · _____
  clothing manufacturer
- [ ] Hired employees (Check the box and see line 12.)
- [ ] Compliance with IRS withholding regulations
- [ ] Other (specify) ·

- [ ] Banking purpose (specify purpose) · _____
- [ ] Changed type of organization (specify new type) · _____
- [ ] Purchased going business
- [ ] Created a trust (specify type) · _____
- [ ] Created a pension plan (specify type) · _____

10 Date business started or acquired (month, day, year)	**11** Closing month of accounting year
10-07-2003	December

12 First date wages or annuities were paid or will be paid (month, day, year). **Note:** *If applicant is a withholding agent, enter date income will first be paid to nonresident alien. (month, day, year)* . . . . · 10-22-2005

13 Highest number of employees expected in the next 12 months. **Note:** *If the applicant does not expect to have any employees during the period, enter "-0-."* . . . . ·

Agricultural	Household	Other
0	0	2

14 Check **one** box that best describes the principal activity of your business.
- [ ] Construction   [ ] Rental & leasing   [ ] Transportation & warehousing   [ ] Health care & social assistance   [ ] Wholesale–agent/broker
- [ ] Real estate   [X] Manufacturing   [ ] Finance & insurance   [ ] Accommodation & food service   [ ] Wholesale–other   [X] Retail
- [ ] Other (specify)

15 Indicate principal line of merchandise sold; specific construction work done; products produced; or services provided.
clothing manufacturer

16a Has the applicant ever applied for an employer identification number for this or any other business? . . . . . [ ] Yes   [ ] No
Note: *If "Yes," please complete lines 16b and 16c.*

16b If you checked "Yes" on line 16a, give applicant's legal name and trade name shown on prior application if different from line 1 or 2 above.
Legal name ·   Trade name ·

16c Approximate date when, and city and state where, the application was filed. Enter previous employer identification number if known.

Approximate date when filed (mo., day, year)	City and state where filed	Previous EIN

Third Party Designee	Complete this section **only** if you want to authorize the named individual to receive the entity's EIN and answer questions about the completion of this form.	
	Designee's name	Designee's telephone number (include area code) ( )
	Address and ZIP code	Designee's fax number (include area code) ( )

Under penalties of perjury, I declare that I have examined this application, and to the best of my knowledge and belief, it is true, correct, and complete.

Name and title (type or print clearly) ·   **Bill Williams, Partner**

Signature ·   *Bill Williams*   Date · *10/15/2003*

Applicant's telephone number (include area code)
(518) 555-0000

Applicant's fax number (include area code)
(518) 555-0001

For Privacy Act and Paperwork Reduction Act Notice, see separate instructions.   Cat. No. 16055N   Form **SS-4** (Rev. 12-2001)

Form **8832**			
(Rev. September 2002) Department of the Treasury Internal Revenue Service	**Entity Classification Election**		OMB No. 1545-1516

	Name of entity		
Type or Print	Williams and Johnson, L.L.C.	EIN ▶	59:12345678
	Number, street, and room or suite no. If a P.O. box, see instructions.		
	123 Liberty Street		
	City or town, state, and ZIP code. If a foreign address, enter city, province or state, postal code and country.		
	Libertyville, FL 33757		

1   Type of election (see instructions):

a ☒ Initial classification by a newly-formed entity.

b ☐ Change in current classification.

2   Form of entity (see instructions):

a ☐ A domestic eligible entity electing to be classified as an association taxable as a corporation.

b ☒ A domestic eligible entity electing to be classified as a partnership.

c ☐ A domestic eligible entity with a single owner electing to be disregarded as a separate entity.

d ☐ A foreign eligible entity electing to be classified as an association taxable as a corporation.

e ☐ A foreign eligible entity electing to be classified as a partnership.

f ☐ A foreign eligible entity with a single owner electing to be disregarded as a separate entity.

3   Disregarded entity information (see instructions):
a Name of owner ▶ ....
b Identifying number of owner ▶ ....
c Country of organization of entity electing to be disregarded (if foreign) ▶ ....

4   Election is to be effective beginning (month, day, year) (see instructions) . . . . ▶ ___ / ___ / ___

5 Name and title of person whom the IRS may call for more information	**6** That person's telephone number
Bill Williams	(909)555-1212

Consent Statement and Signature(s) (see instructions)

Under penalties of perjury, I (we) declare that I (we) consent to the election of the above-named entity to be classified as indicated above, and that I (we) have examined this consent statement, and to the best of my (our) knowledge and belief, it is true, correct, and complete. If I am an officer, manager, or member signing for all members of the entity, I further declare that I am authorized to execute this consent statement on their behalf.

Signature(s)	Date	Title
Bill Williams	*Oct. 15, 2005*	Member
John Johnson	*Oct. 15, 2005*	Member

For Paperwork Reduction Act Notice, see page 4.   Cat. No. 22598R   Form **8832** (Rev. 9-2002)

BILL OF SALE

The undersigned, in consideration of membership interest in _____ Galt Industries, L.L.C. _____

_____, a _____ Colorado _____ limited liability company, hereby grants, bar-

gains, sells, transfers, and delivers unto said corporation the following goods and chattels:

A 1997 Ford panel truck, VIN 1234567890 valued at $12,600
a G&R industrial lathe, Model 605 valued at $2,800

To have and to hold the same forever.

And the undersigned, their heirs, successors, and administrators, covenant and warrant that they are the lawful

owners of the said goods and chattels and that they are free from all encumbrances. That the undersigned have the

right to sell this property and that they will warrant and defend the sale of said property against the lawful claims

and demands of all persons.

IN WITNESS whereof the undersigned have executed this Bill of Sale this __1__ day of _____ May _____,

__2006__ .

_____ *John Galt* _____
John Galt

_____

_____

SCHEDULE A
TO LIMITED LIABILITY COMPANY
OPERATING OR MANAGEMENT AGREEMENT OF
Williams and Johnson, L.L.C.

1. Initial member(s): The initial member(s) are:

Bill Willliams, 123 Liberty Street, Libertyville, FL 33757

John Johnson, 605 Galt Street, Libertyville, FL 33757

2. Capital Contribution(s): The capital contribution(s) of the member(s) is/are:

Bill Willliams, $5,000 cash

John Johnson, $2,000 cash, 2002 GMC truck valued at $3,000

3. Profits and Losses: The profits, losses, and other tax matters shall be allocated among the members in the following percentages:

Bill Willliams, 50%

John Johnson, 50%

4. Management: The company shall be managed by:

Bill Willliams, 123 Liberty Street, Libertyville, FL 33757

John Johnson, 605 Galt Street, Libertyville, FL 33757

5. Registered Agent: The initial registered agent and registered office of the company are:

Bill Willliams, 123 Liberty Street, Libertyville, FL 33757

John Johnson, 605 Galt Street, Libertyville, FL 33757

6. The tax matters partner is:

Bill Willliams

MINUTES OF A MEETING OF MEMBERS OF

Williams and Johnson, L.L.C.

A meeting of the members of the company was held on ___May 2, 2006___ , at
___123 Liberty Street, Libertyville, FL 33757___ .

The following were present, being all the members of the limited liability company:
___Bill Williams___   ___John Johnson___

The meeting was called to order and it was moved, seconded, and unanimously carried that
___Bill Williams___ act as Chairman and that ___John Johnson___ act as Secretary.

After discussion and upon motion duly made, seconded, and carried the following resolution(s) were adopted:

The company agreed to buy a warehouse on Highway 31 in Libertyville and to finance
it it with a loan of $120,000 borrowed from Liberty Bank at 9% interest payable over 20
years.

There being no further business to come before the meeting, upon motion duly made, seconded, and unanimously carried, it was adjourned.

John Johnson
Secretary

Members:

Bill Williams

John Johnson

CERTIFICATE OF AUTHORITY
FOR
Williams and Johnson, L.L.C.

This is to certify that the above limited liability company is managed by its

☒ members

❑ managers

who are listed below and that each of them is authorized and empowered to transact business on behalf of the company.

Name   Address

_____ Bill Williams _____   _____ 123 Liberty Street _____

                                              _____ Libertyville, FL 33757 _____

_____ John Johnson _____   _____ 605 Galt Street _____

                                              _____ Libertyville, FL 33757 _____

_____   _____

_____   _____

                                              _____

Date: _____ May 29, 2006 _____

Name of company:
_____ Williams and Johnson, L.L.C. _____
By: _Bill Williams_____
Bill Williams
Position: _Member_____

BANKING RESOLUTION OF

Williams and Johnson, L.L.C.

The undersigned, being a member of the above limited liability company authorized to sigh this resolution, hereby certifies that on the __6__ day of __June__, __2006__ the members of the limited liability company adopted the following resolution:

RESOLVED that the limited liability company open bank accounts with __Liberty Bank__ and that the members of the company are authorized to take such action as is necessary to open such accounts; that the bank's printed form of resolution is hereby adopted and incorporated into these minutes by reference; and, that any __1__ of the following person(s) shall have signature authority over the account:

__Bill Williams__   __John Johnson__

_____   _____ ;

and, that said resolution has not been modified or rescinded.

Date: __June 6, 2006__

Bill Williams
Authorized member

Appendix C: Blank Forms

TRANSMITTAL LETTER

To:

Re:

Enclosed is an original and _____ copies of Articles of Organization for the above-referenced LLC along with a check for $_____ as follows:

> $_____   for filing fee
>
> $_____   for _____

Please send acknowledgement of receipt and/or date-stamped copy to:

This page intentionally left blank.

ARTICLES OF ORGANIZATION FOR A LIMITED LIABILITY COMPANY

ARTICLE I - Name:

The name of the Limited Liability Company is:

ARTICLE II - Purpose:

The purpose for which this limited liability company is organized is:

ARTICLE III - Duration:

The period of duration for the Limited Liability Company shall be:

ARTICLE IV - Registered (or Statutory) Agent and Address:

The name and address of the initial registered (statutory) agent is:

ARTICLE V - Management:
(Check the appropriate box and complete the statement)

❑ The Limited Liability Company is to be managed by a manager or managers and the name(s) and address(es) of such manager(s) who is/are to serve as manager(s) is/are:

❑ The Limited Liability Company is to be managed by the members and the name(s) and address(es) of the managing members is/are:

ARTICLE VI - Principal Place of Business

The initial principal place of business of the Limited Liability Company is:

ARTICLE VII - Effective Date

The effective date of these articles is ❑ upon filing ❑ on _____

ARTICLE VIII - Nonliability

The members and managers, if any, shall not be liable for any debts, obligations, or liabilities of the limited liability company.

ARTICLE IX - Miscellaneous

IN WITNESS WHEREOF the undersigned members executed these Articles of Organization this _____ day of
_____, _____.

_____
Member: Address:

_____
Member: Address:

_____
Member: Address:

_____
Member: Address:

Acceptance of Registered (Statutory) Agent

Having been named as registered agent and to accept service of process for the above stated limited liability company at the place designated in this certificate, I hereby accept the appointment as registered agent and agree to act in this capacity. I further agree to comply with the provisions of all statutes relating to the proper and complete performance of my duties, and am familiar with and accept the obligations of my position as registered agent.

_____
Agent:

Form **SS-4**

(Rev. December 2001)

Department of the Treasury
Internal Revenue Service

Application for Employer Identification Number

(For use by employers, corporations, partnerships, trusts, estates, churches, government agencies, Indian tribal entities, certain individuals, and others.)

· See separate instructions for each line. · Keep a copy for your records.

Form 3   209

EIN

OMB No. 1545-0003

Type or print clearly.

1 Legal name of entity (or individual) for whom the EIN is being requested

2 Trade name of business (if different from name on line 1)

3 Executor, trustee, "care of" name

4a Mailing address (room, apt., suite no. and street, or P.O. box)

5a Street address (if different) (Do not enter a P.O. box.)

4b City, state, and ZIP code

5b City, state, and ZIP code

6 County and state where principal business is located

7a Name of principal officer, general partner, grantor, owner, or trustor

7b SSN, ITIN, or EIN

8a **Type of entity** (check only one box)

- ☐ Sole proprietor (SSN) _____
- ☐ Partnership
- ☐ Corporation (enter form number to be filed) · _____
- ☐ Personal service corp.
- ☐ Church or church-controlled organization
- ☐ Other nonprofit organization (specify) · _____
- ☐ Other (specify) · _____

- ☐ Estate (SSN of decedent) _____
- ☐ Plan administrator (SSN) _____
- ☐ Trust (SSN of grantor) _____
- ☐ National Guard   ☐ State/local government
- ☐ Farmers' cooperative   ☐ Federal government/military
- ☐ REMIC   ☐ Indian tribal governments/enterprises

Group Exemption Number (GEN) · _____

8b If a corporation, name the state or foreign country (if applicable) where incorporated

State

Foreign country

9 **Reason for applying** (check only one box)

- ☐ Started new business (specify type) · _____
- ☐ Hired employees (Check the box and see line 12.)
- ☐ Compliance with IRS withholding regulations
- ☐ Other (specify) · _____

- ☐ Banking purpose (specify purpose) · _____
- ☐ Changed type of organization (specify new type) · _____
- ☐ Purchased going business
- ☐ Created a trust (specify type) · _____
- ☐ Created a pension plan (specify type) · _____

10 Date business started or acquired (month, day, year)

11 Closing month of accounting year

12 First date wages or annuities were paid or will be paid (month, day, year). **Note:** *If applicant is a withholding agent, enter date income will first be paid to nonresident alien. (month, day, year)* . . . . ·

13 Highest number of employees expected in the next 12 months. **Note:** *If the applicant does not expect to have any employees during the period, enter "-0-."* . . . .

Agricultural	Household	Other

14 Check **one** box that best describes the principal activity of your business.

- ☐ Construction
- ☐ Real estate
- ☐ Rental & leasing
- ☐ Manufacturing
- ☐ Transportation & warehousing
- ☐ Finance & insurance
- ☐ Health care & social assistance
- ☐ Accommodation & food service
- ☐ Other (specify)
- ☐ Wholesale–agent/broker
- ☐ Wholesale–other
- ☐ Retail

15 Indicate principal line of merchandise sold; specific construction work done; products produced; or services provided.

16a Has the applicant ever applied for an employer identification number for this or any other business? . . . . . ☐ **Yes** ☐ **No**

Note: *If "Yes," please complete lines 16b and 16c.*

16b If you checked "Yes" on line 16a, give applicant's legal name and trade name shown on prior application if different from line 1 or 2 above.

Legal name ·   Trade name ·

16c Approximate date when, and city and state where, the application was filed. Enter previous employer identification number if known.

Approximate date when filed (mo., day, year)   City and state where filed   Previous EIN

Third Party Designee

Complete this section **only** if you want to authorize the named individual to receive the entity's EIN and answer questions about the completion of this form.

Designee's name

Designee's telephone number (include area code)
( )

Address and ZIP code

Designee's fax number (include area code)
( )

Under penalties of perjury, I declare that I have examined this application, and to the best of my knowledge and belief, it is true, correct, and complete.

Applicant's telephone number (include area code)
( )

Name and title (type or print clearly) ·

Applicant's fax number (include area code)
( )

Signature ·   Date ·

For Privacy Act and Paperwork Reduction Act Notice, see separate instructions.   Cat. No. 16055N   Form **SS-4** (Rev. 12-2001)

210

Instructions for Form SS-4
(Rev. September 2003)

Department of the Treasury
Internal Revenue Service

For use with Form SS-4 (Rev. December 2001)
Application for Employer Identification Number.

Section references are to the Internal Revenue Code unless otherwise noted.

General Instructions

Use these instructions to complete **Form SS-4,**
Application for Employer Identification Number. Also see
Do I Need an EIN? on page 2 of Form SS-4.

Purpose of Form

Use Form SS-4 to apply for an employer identification
number (EIN). An EIN is a nine-digit number (for
example, 12-3456789) assigned to sole proprietors,
corporations, partnerships, estates, trusts, and other
entities for tax filing and reporting purposes. The
information you provide on this form will establish your
business tax account.

 *An EIN is for use in connection with your
business activities only. Do **not** use your EIN in
place of your social security number (SSN).*

Items To Note

Apply online. You can now apply for and receive an EIN
online using the internet. See **How To Apply** below.

File only one Form SS-4. Generally, a sole proprietor
should file only one Form SS-4 and needs only one EIN,
regardless of the number of businesses operated as a
sole proprietorship or trade names under which a
business operates. However, if the proprietorship
incorporates or enters into a partnership, a new EIN is
required. Also, each corporation in an affiliated group
must have its own EIN.

EIN applied for, but not received. If you do not have an
EIN by the time a return is due, write "Applied For" and
the date you applied in the space shown for the number.
Do not show your SSN as an EIN on returns.

If you do not have an EIN by the time a tax deposit is
due, send your payment to the Internal Revenue Service
Center for your filing area as shown in the instructions for
the form that you are filing. Make your check or money
order payable to the "United States Treasury" and show
your name (as shown on Form SS-4), address, type of
tax, period covered, and date you applied for an EIN.

How To Apply

You can apply for an EIN online, by telephone, by fax, or
by mail depending on how soon you need to use the EIN.
Use only one method for each entity so you do not
receive more than one EIN for an entity.

Online. You can receive your EIN by internet and use it
immediately to file a return or make a payment. Go to the

IRS website at **www.irs.gov/businesses** and click on
Employer ID Numbers under **topics.**

Telephone. You can receive your EIN by telephone and
use it immediately to file a return or make a payment.
Call the IRS at **1-800-829-4933.** (International applicants
must call 215-516-6999.) The hours of operation are 7:00
a.m. to 10:00 p.m. The person making the call must be
authorized to sign the form or be an authorized designee.
See **Signature** and **Third Party Designee** on page 6.
Also see the **TIP** below.

If you are applying by telephone, it will be helpful to
complete Form SS-4 before contacting the IRS. An IRS
representative will use the information from the Form
SS-4 to establish your account and assign you an EIN.
Write the number you are given on the upper right corner
of the form and sign and date it. Keep this copy for your
records.

If requested by an IRS representative, mail or fax
(facsimile) the signed Form SS-4 (including any Third
Party Designee authorization) within 24 hours to the IRS
address provided by the IRS representative.

 *Taxpayer representatives can apply for an EIN
on behalf of their client and request that the
EIN be faxed to their **client** on the same day.
Note: By using this procedure, you are
authorizing the IRS to fax the EIN without a cover sheet.*

Fax. Under the Fax-TIN program, you can receive your
EIN by fax within 4 business days. Complete and fax
Form SS-4 to the IRS using the Fax-TIN number listed on
page 2 for your state. A long-distance charge to callers
outside of the local calling area will apply. Fax-TIN
numbers can only be used to apply for an EIN. **The
numbers may change without notice.** Fax-TIN is
available 24 hours a day, 7 days a week.

Be sure to provide your fax number so the IRS can fax
the EIN back to you. **Note:** By using this procedure, you
are authorizing the IRS to fax the EIN without a cover
sheet.

Mail. Complete Form SS-4 at least 4 to 5 weeks before
you will need an EIN. Sign and date the application and
mail it to the service center address for your state. You
will receive your EIN in the mail in approximately 4
weeks. See also **Third Party Designee** on page 6.

**Call 1-800-829-4933 to verify a number or to ask
about the status of an application by mail.**

Cat. No. 62736F

Where To Fax or File

If your principal business, office or agency, or legal residence in the case of an individual, is located in:	Call the Fax-TIN number shown or file with the "Internal Revenue Service Center" at:
Connecticut, Delaware, District of Columbia, Florida, Georgia, Maine, Maryland, Massachusetts, New Hampshire, New Jersey, New York, North Carolina, Ohio, Pennsylvania, Rhode Island, South Carolina, Vermont, Virginia, West Virginia	Attn: EIN Operation P. O. Box 9003 Holtsville, NY 11742-9003 Fax-TIN 631-447-8960
Illinois, Indiana, Kentucky, Michigan	Attn: EIN Operation Cincinnati, OH 45999 Fax-TIN 859-669-5760
Alabama, Alaska, Arizona, Arkansas, California, Colorado, Hawaii, Idaho, Iowa, Kansas, Louisiana, Minnesota, Mississippi, Missouri, Montana, Nebraska, Nevada, New Mexico, North Dakota, Oklahoma, Oregon, Puerto Rico, South Dakota, Tennessee, Texas, Utah, Washington, Wisconsin, Wyoming	Attn: EIN Operation Philadelphia, PA 19255 Fax-TIN 215-516-3990
If you have no legal residence, principal place of business, or principal office or agency in any state:	Attn: EIN Operation Philadelphia, PA 19255 Telephone 215-516-6999 Fax-TIN 215-516-3990

How To Get Forms and Publications

Phone. You can order forms, instructions, and publications by phone 24 hours a day, 7 days a week. Call 1-800-TAX-FORM (1-800-829-3676). You should receive your order or notification of its status within 10 workdays.

Personal computer. With your personal computer and modem, you can get the forms and information you need using the IRS website at **www.irs.gov** or File Transfer Protocol at **ftp.irs.gov.**

CD-ROM. For small businesses, return preparers, or others who may frequently need tax forms or publications, a CD-ROM containing over 2,000 tax products (including many prior year forms) can be purchased from the National Technical Information Service (NTIS).

To order **Pub. 1796,** Federal Tax Products on CD-ROM, call **1-877-CDFORMS** (1-877-233-6767) toll free or connect to **www.irs.gov/cdorders.**

Tax Help for Your Business

IRS-sponsored Small Business Workshops provide information about your Federal and state tax obligations.

For information about workshops in your area, call 1-800-829-4933.

Related Forms and Publications

The following **forms** and **instructions** may be useful to filers of Form SS-4:
* **Form 990-T,** Exempt Organization Business Income Tax Return
* **Instructions for Form 990-T**
* **Schedule C (Form 1040),** Profit or Loss From Business
* **Schedule F (Form 1040),** Profit or Loss From Farming
* **Instructions for Form 1041 and Schedules A, B, D, G, I, J, and K-1,** U.S. Income Tax Return for Estates and Trusts
* **Form 1042,** Annual Withholding Tax Return for U.S. Source Income of Foreign Persons
* **Instructions for Form 1065,** U.S. Return of Partnership Income
* **Instructions for Form 1066,** U.S. Real Estate Mortgage Investment Conduit (REMIC) Income Tax Return
* **Instructions for Forms 1120 and 1120-A**
* **Form 2553,** Election by a Small Business Corporation
* **Form 2848,** Power of Attorney and Declaration of Representative
* **Form 8821,** Tax Information Authorization
* **Form 8832,** Entity Classification Election
    For more **information** about filing Form SS-4 and related issues, see:
* **Circular A,** Agricultural Employer's Tax Guide (Pub. 51)
* **Circular E,** Employer's Tax Guide (Pub. 15)
* **Pub. 538,** Accounting Periods and Methods
* **Pub. 542,** Corporations
* **Pub. 557,** Exempt Status for Your Organization
* **Pub. 583,** Starting a Business and Keeping Records
* **Pub. 966,** Electronic Choices for Paying ALL Your Federal Taxes
* **Pub. 1635,** Understanding Your EIN
* **Package 1023,** Application for Recognition of Exemption Under Section 501(c)(3) of the Internal Revenue Code
* **Package 1024,** Application for Recognition of Exemption Under Section 501(a)

Specific Instructions

Print or type all entries on Form SS-4. Follow the instructions for each line to expedite processing and to avoid unnecessary IRS requests for additional information. Enter "N/A" (nonapplicable) on the lines that do not apply.

Line 1—Legal name of entity (or individual) for whom the EIN is being requested. Enter the legal name of the entity (or individual) applying for the EIN exactly as it appears on the social security card, charter, or other applicable legal document.

Individuals. Enter your first name, middle initial, and last name. If you are a sole proprietor, enter your individual name, not your business name. Enter your business name on line 2. Do not use abbreviations or nicknames on line 1.

Trusts. Enter the name of the trust.

Estate of a decedent. Enter the name of the estate.

Partnerships. Enter the legal name of the partnership as it appears in the partnership agreement.

Corporations. Enter the corporate name as it appears in the corporation charter or other legal document creating it.

Plan administrators. Enter the name of the plan administrator. A plan administrator who already has an EIN should use that number.

Line 2—Trade name of business. Enter the trade name of the business if different from the legal name. The trade name is the "doing business as " (DBA) name.

 *Use the full legal name shown on line 1 on all tax returns filed for the entity. (However, if you enter a trade name on line 2 and choose to use the trade name instead of the legal name, enter the trade name on **all returns** you file.) To prevent processing delays and errors, **always** use the legal name only (or the trade name only) on **all** tax returns.*

Line 3—Executor, trustee, "care of" name. Trusts enter the name of the trustee. Estates enter the name of the executor, administrator, or other fiduciary. If the entity applying has a designated person to receive tax information, enter that person's name as the "care of" person. Enter the individual's first name, middle initial, and last name.

Lines 4a-b—Mailing address. Enter the mailing address for the entity's correspondence. If line 3 is completed, enter the address for the executor, trustee or "care of" person. Generally, this address will be used on all tax returns.

 *File **Form 8822**, Change of Address, to report any subsequent changes to the entity's mailing address.*

Lines 5a-b—Street address. Provide the entity's physical address **only** if different from its mailing address shown in lines 4a-b. **Do not** enter a P.O. box number here.

Line 6—County and state where principal business is located. Enter the entity's primary **physical** location.

Lines 7a-b—Name of principal officer, general partner, grantor, owner, or trustor. Enter the first name, middle initial, last name, and SSN of **(a)** the principal officer if the business is a corporation, **(b)** a general partner if a partnership, **(c)** the owner of an entity that is disregarded as separate from its owner (disregarded entities owned by a corporation enter the corporation's name and EIN), or **(d)** a grantor, owner, or trustor if a trust.

If the person in question is an **alien individual** with a previously assigned individual taxpayer identification number (ITIN), enter the ITIN in the space provided and submit a copy of an official identifying document. If

necessary, complete **Form W-7,** Application for IRS Individual Taxpayer Identification Number, to obtain an ITIN.

You are **required** to enter an SSN, ITIN, or EIN unless the only reason you are applying for an EIN is to make an entity classification election (see Regulations sections 301.7701-1 through 301.7701-3) and you are a nonresident alien with no effectively connected income from sources within the United States.

Line 8a—Type of entity. Check the box that best describes the type of entity applying for the EIN. If you are an alien individual with an ITIN previously assigned to you, enter the ITIN in place of a requested SSN.

 *This is not an election for a tax classification of an entity. See **Limited liability company (LLC)** on page 4.*

Other. If not specifically listed, check the "Other" box, enter the type of entity and the type of return, if any, that will be filed (for example, "Common Trust Fund, Form 1065" or "Created a Pension Plan"). Do not enter "N/A." If you are an alien individual applying for an EIN, see the **Lines 7a-b** instructions above.

● **Household employer.** If you are an individual, check the "Other" box and enter "Household Employer" and your SSN. If you are a state or local agency serving as a tax reporting agent for public assistance recipients who become household employers, check the "Other" box and enter "Household Employer Agent." If you are a trust that qualifies as a household employer, you do not need a separate EIN for reporting tax information relating to household employees; use the EIN of the trust.

● **QSub.** For a qualified subchapter S subsidiary (QSub) check the "Other" box and specify "QSub."

● **Withholding agent.** If you are a withholding agent required to file Form 1042, check the "Other" box and enter "Withholding Agent."

Sole proprietor. Check this box if you file Schedule C, C-EZ, or F (Form 1040) and have a qualified plan, or are required to file excise, employment, alcohol, tobacco, or firearms returns, or are a payer of gambling winnings. Enter your SSN (or ITIN) in the space provided. If you are a nonresident alien with no effectively connected income from sources within the United States, you do not need to enter an SSN or ITIN.

Corporation. This box is for any corporation **other than a personal service corporation.** If you check this box, enter the income tax form number to be filed by the entity in the space provided.

 *If you entered "1120S" after the "Corporation" checkbox, the corporation **must** file Form 2553 **no later than the 15th day of the 3rd month of the tax year the election is to take effect.** Until Form 2553 has been received and approved, you will be considered a Form 1120 filer. See the Instructions for Form 2553.*

Personal service corp. Check this box if the entity is a personal service corporation. An entity is a personal service corporation for a tax year only if:

• The principal activity of the entity during the testing period (prior tax year) for the tax year is the performance of personal services substantially by employee-owners, and

• The employee-owners own at least 10% of the fair market value of the outstanding stock in the entity on the last day of the testing period.

Personal services include performance of services in such fields as health, law, accounting, or consulting. For more information about personal service corporations, see the Instructions for Forms 1120 and 1120-A and Pub. 542.

Other nonprofit organization. Check this box if the nonprofit organization is other than a church or church-controlled organization and specify the type of nonprofit organization (for example, an educational organization).

 *If the organization also seeks tax-exempt status, you **must** file either Package 1023 or Package 1024. See Pub. 557 for more information.*

If the organization is covered by a group exemption letter, enter the four-digit **group exemption number (GEN).** (Do not confuse the GEN with the nine-digit EIN.) If you do not know the GEN, contact the parent organization. Get Pub. 557 for more information about group exemption numbers.

Plan administrator. If the plan administrator is an individual, enter the plan administrator's SSN in the space provided.

REMIC. Check this box if the entity has elected to be treated as a real estate mortgage investment conduit (REMIC). See the Instructions for Form 1066 for more information.

Limited liability company (LLC). An LLC is an entity organized under the laws of a state or foreign country as a limited liability company. For Federal tax purposes, an LLC may be treated as a partnership or corporation or be disregarded as an entity separate from its owner.

By **default,** a domestic LLC with only one member is **disregarded** as an entity separate from its owner and must include all of its income and expenses on the owner's tax return (e.g., **Schedule C (Form 1040)**). Also by default, a domestic LLC with two or more members is treated as a partnership. A domestic LLC may file Form 8832 to avoid either default classification and elect to be classified as an association taxable as a corporation. For more information on entity classifications (including the rules for foreign entities), see the instructions for Form 8832.

 *Do not file Form 8832 if the LLC accepts the default classifications above. **However, if the LLC will be electing S Corporation status, it must timely file both Form 8832 and Form 2553.***

Complete Form SS-4 for LLCs as follows:
• A single-member domestic LLC that accepts the default classification (above) does not need an EIN and generally should not file Form SS-4. Generally, the LLC

should use the name and EIN of its **owner** for all Federal tax purposes. However, the reporting and payment of employment taxes for employees of the LLC may be made using the name and EIN of **either** the owner or the LLC as explained in Notice 99-6. You can find Notice 99-6 on page 12 of Internal Revenue Bulletin 1999-3 at **www.irs.gov/pub/irs-irbs/irb99-03.pdf. (Note:** If the LLC applicant indicates in box 13 that it has employees or expects to have employees, the owner (whether an individual or other entity) of a single-member domestic LLC will also be assigned its own EIN (if it does not already have one) even if the LLC will be filing the employment tax returns.)

• A single-member, domestic LLC that accepts the default classification (above) and wants an EIN for filing employment tax returns (see above) or non-Federal purposes, such as a state requirement, must check the "Other" box and write "Disregarded Entity" or, when applicable, "Disregarded Entity—Sole Proprietorship" in the space provided.

• A multi-member, domestic LLC that accepts the default classification (above) must check the "Partnership" box.

• A domestic LLC that will be filing Form 8832 to elect corporate status must check the "Corporation" box and write in "Single-Member" or "Multi-Member" immediately below the "form number" entry line.

Line 9—Reason for applying. Check only **one** box. Do not enter "N/A."

Started new business. Check this box if you are starting a new business that requires an EIN. If you check this box, enter the type of business being started. **Do not** apply if you already have an EIN and are only adding another place of business.

Hired employees. Check this box if the existing business is requesting an EIN because it has hired or is hiring employees and is therefore required to file employment tax returns. **Do not** apply if you already have an EIN and are only hiring employees. For information on employment taxes (e.g., for family members), see Circular E.

 You may be required to make electronic deposits of all depository taxes (such as employment tax, excise tax, and corporate income tax) using the Electronic Federal Tax Payment System (EFTPS). See section 11, Depositing Taxes, of Circular E and Pub. 966.

Created a pension plan. Check this box if you have created a pension plan and need an EIN for reporting purposes. Also, enter the type of plan in the space provided.

 Check this box if you are applying for a trust EIN when a new pension plan is established. In addition, check the "Other" box in line 8a and write "Created a Pension Plan" in the space provided.

Banking purpose. Check this box if you are requesting an EIN for banking purposes only, and enter the banking purpose (for example, a bowling league for depositing dues or an investment club for dividend and interest reporting).

Changed type of organization. Check this box if the business is changing its type of organization. For example, the business was a sole proprietorship and has been incorporated or has become a partnership. If you check this box, specify in the space provided (including available space immediately below) the type of change made. For example, "From Sole Proprietorship to Partnership."

Purchased going business. Check this box if you purchased an existing business. **Do not** use the former owner's EIN unless you became the "owner" of a corporation by acquiring its stock.

Created a trust. Check this box if you created a trust, and enter the type of trust created. For example, indicate if the trust is a nonexempt charitable trust or a split-interest trust.

Exception. Do **not** file this form for certain grantor-type trusts. The trustee does not need an EIN for the trust if the trustee furnishes the name and TIN of the grantor/owner and the address of the trust to all payors. See the Instructions for Form 1041 for more information.

 Do not *check this box if you are applying for a trust EIN when a new pension plan is established. Check "Created a pension plan."*

Other. Check this box if you are requesting an EIN for any other reason; and enter the reason. For example, a newly-formed state government entity should enter "Newly-Formed State Government Entity" in the space provided.

Line 10—Date business started or acquired. If you are starting a new business, enter the starting date of the business. If the business you acquired is already operating, enter the date you acquired the business. If you are changing the form of ownership of your business, enter the date the new ownership entity began. Trusts should enter the date the trust was legally created. Estates should enter the date of death of the decedent whose name appears on line 1 or the date when the estate was legally funded.

Line 11—Closing month of accounting year. Enter the last month of your accounting year or tax year. An accounting or tax year is usually 12 consecutive months, either a calendar year or a fiscal year (including a period of 52 or 53 weeks). A calendar year is 12 consecutive months ending on December 31. A fiscal year is either 12 consecutive months ending on the last day of any month other than December or a 52-53 week year. For more information on accounting periods, see Pub. 538.

Individuals. Your tax year generally will be a calendar year.

Partnerships. Partnerships must adopt one of the following tax years:
• The tax year of the majority of its partners,
• The tax year common to all of its principal partners,
• The tax year that results in the least aggregate deferral of income, or
• In certain cases, some other tax year.

See the Instructions for Form 1065 for more information.

REMICs. REMICs must have a calendar year as their tax year.

Personal service corporations. A personal service corporation generally must adopt a calendar year unless:
• It can establish a business purpose for having a different tax year, or
• It elects under section 444 to have a tax year other than a calendar year.

Trusts. Generally, a trust must adopt a calendar year except for the following:
• Tax-exempt trusts,
• Charitable trusts, and
• Grantor-owned trusts.

Line 12—First date wages or annuities were paid or will be paid. If the business has or will have employees, enter the date on which the business began or will begin to pay wages. If the business does not plan to have employees, enter "N/A."

Withholding agent. Enter the date you began or will begin to pay income (including annuities) to a nonresident alien. This also applies to individuals who are required to file Form 1042 to report alimony paid to a nonresident alien.

Line 13—Highest number of employees expected in the next 12 months. Complete each box by entering the number (including zero ("-0-")) of "Agricultural," "Household," or "Other" employees expected by the applicant in the next 12 months. For a definition of agricultural labor (farmwork), see Circular A.

Lines 14 and 15. Check the **one** box in line 14 that best describes the principal activity of the applicant's business. Check the "Other" box (and specify the applicant's principal activity) if none of the listed boxes applies.

Use line 15 to describe the applicant's principal line of business in more detail. For example, if you checked the "Construction" box in line 14, enter additional detail such as "General contractor for residential buildings" in line 15.

Construction. Check this box if the applicant is engaged in erecting buildings or other structures, (e.g., streets, highways, bridges, tunnels). The term "Construction" also includes special trade contractors, (e.g., plumbing, HVAC, electrical, carpentry, concrete, excavation, etc. contractors).

Real estate. Check this box if the applicant is engaged in renting or leasing real estate to others; managing, selling, buying or renting real estate for others; or providing related real estate services (e.g., appraisal services).

Rental and leasing. Check this box if the applicant is engaged in providing tangible goods such as autos, computers, consumer goods, or industrial machinery and equipment to customers in return for a periodic rental or lease payment.

Manufacturing. Check this box if the applicant is engaged in the mechanical, physical, or chemical transformation of materials, substances, or components into new products. The assembling of component parts of manufactured products is also considered to be manufacturing.

Transportation & warehousing. Check this box if the applicant provides transportation of passengers or cargo; warehousing or storage of goods; scenic or sight-seeing transportation; or support activities related to these modes of transportation.

Finance & insurance. Check this box if the applicant is engaged in transactions involving the creation, liquidation, or change of ownership of financial assets and/or facilitating such financial transactions; underwriting annuities/insurance policies; facilitating such underwriting by selling insurance policies; or by providing other insurance or employee-benefit related services.

Health care and social assistance. Check this box if the applicant is engaged in providing physical, medical, or psychiatric care using licensed health care professionals or providing social assistance activities such as youth centers, adoption agencies, individual/ family services, temporary shelters, etc.

Accommodation & food services. Check this box if the applicant is engaged in providing customers with lodging, meal preparation, snacks, or beverages for immediate consumption.

Wholesale–agent/broker. Check this box if the applicant is engaged in arranging for the purchase or sale of goods owned by others or purchasing goods on a commission basis for goods traded in the wholesale market, usually between businesses.

Wholesale–other. Check this box if the applicant is engaged in selling goods in the wholesale market generally to other businesses for resale on their own account.

Retail. Check this box if the applicant is engaged in selling merchandise to the general public from a fixed store; by direct, mail-order, or electronic sales; or by using vending machines.

Other. Check this box if the applicant is engaged in an activity not described above. Describe the applicant's principal business activity in the space provided.

Lines 16a–c. Check the applicable box in line 16a to indicate whether or not the entity (or individual) applying for an EIN was issued one previously. Complete lines 16b and 16c **only** if the "Yes" box in line 16a is checked. If the applicant previously applied for **more than one** EIN, write "See Attached" in the empty space in line 16a and attach a separate sheet providing the line 16b and 16c information for each EIN previously requested.

Third Party Designee. Complete this section **only** if you want to authorize the named individual to receive the entity's EIN and answer questions about the completion of Form SS-4. The designee's authority terminates at the time the EIN is assigned and released to the designee. **You must complete the signature area for the authorization to be valid.**

Signature. When required, the application must be signed by **(a)** the individual, if the applicant is an individual, **(b)** the president, vice president, or other principal officer, if the applicant is a corporation, **(c)** a responsible and duly authorized member or officer having knowledge of its affairs, if the applicant is a partnership, government entity, or other unincorporated organization, or **(d)** the fiduciary, if the applicant is a trust or an estate. Foreign applicants may have any duly-authorized person, (e.g., division manager), sign Form SS-4.

Privacy Act and Paperwork Reduction Act Notice. We ask for the information on this form to carry out the Internal Revenue laws of the United States. We need it to comply with section 6109 and the regulations thereunder which generally require the inclusion of an employer identification number (EIN) on certain returns, statements, or other documents filed with the Internal Revenue Service. If your entity is required to obtain an EIN, you are required to provide all of the information requested on this form. Information on this form may be used to determine which Federal tax returns you are required to file and to provide you with related forms and publications.

We disclose this form to the Social Security Administration for their use in determining compliance with applicable laws. We may give this information to the Department of Justice for use in civil and criminal litigation, and to the cities, states, and the District of Columbia for use in administering their tax laws. We may also disclose this information to Federal and state agencies to enforce Federal nontax criminal laws and to combat terrorism.

We will be unable to issue an EIN to you unless you provide all of the requested information which applies to your entity. Providing false information could subject you to penalties.

You are not required to provide the information requested on a form that is subject to the Paperwork Reduction Act unless the form displays a valid OMB control number. Books or records relating to a form or its instructions must be retained as long as their contents may become material in the administration of any Internal Revenue law. Generally, tax returns and return information are confidential, as required by section 6103.

The time needed to complete and file this form will vary depending on individual circumstances. The estimated average time is:

Recordkeeping	6 min.
Learning about the law or the form	22 min.
Preparing the form	46 min.
Copying, assembling, and sending the form to the IRS	20 min.

If you have comments concerning the accuracy of these time estimates or suggestions for making this form simpler, we would be happy to hear from you. You can write to the Tax Products Coordinating Committee, Western Area Distribution Center, Rancho Cordova, CA 95743-0001. **Do not** send the form to this address. Instead, see **How To Apply** on page 1.

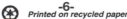

This page intentionally left blank.

Form 8832
(Rev. September 2002)
Department of the Treasury
Internal Revenue Service

Entity Classification Election

OMB No. 1545-1516

Type or Print	Name of entity	EIN ▶
	Number, street, and room or suite no. If a P.O. box, see instructions.	
	City or town, state, and ZIP code. If a foreign address, enter city, province or state, postal code and country.	

1   Type of election (see instructions):

a ☐ Initial classification by a newly-formed entity.

b ☐ Change in current classification.

2   Form of entity (see instructions):

a ☐ A domestic eligible entity electing to be classified as an association taxable as a corporation.

b ☐ A domestic eligible entity electing to be classified as a partnership.

c ☐ A domestic eligible entity with a single owner electing to be disregarded as a separate entity.

d ☐ A foreign eligible entity electing to be classified as an association taxable as a corporation.

e ☐ A foreign eligible entity electing to be classified as a partnership.

f ☐ A foreign eligible entity with a single owner electing to be disregarded as a separate entity.

3   Disregarded entity information (see instructions):
a Name of owner ▶ ....
b Identifying number of owner ▶ ....
c Country of organization of entity electing to be disregarded (if foreign) ▶ ....

4   Election is to be effective beginning (month, day, year) (see instructions)   . . . . ▶ ___ / ___ / ___

5   Name and title of person whom the IRS may call for more information

6   That person's telephone number
(   )

Consent Statement and Signature(s) (see instructions)

Under penalties of perjury, I (we) declare that I (we) consent to the election of the above-named entity to be classified as indicated above, and that I (we) have examined this consent statement, and to the best of my (our) knowledge and belief, it is true, correct, and complete. If I am an officer, manager, or member signing for all members of the entity, I further declare that I am authorized to execute this consent statement on their behalf.

Signature(s)	Date	Title

For Paperwork Reduction Act Notice, see page 4.   Cat. No. 22598R   Form **8832** (Rev. 9-2002)

218

General Instructions

Section references are to the Internal Revenue Code unless otherwise noted.

Purpose of Form

For Federal tax purposes, certain business entities automatically are classified as corporations. See items **1** and **3** through **8** under the definition of **corporation** on this page. Other business entities may choose how they are classified for Federal tax purposes. Except for a business entity automatically classified as a corporation, a business entity with at least two members can choose to be classified as either an association taxable as a corporation or a partnership, and a business entity with a single member can choose to be classified as either an association taxable as a corporation or disregarded as an entity separate from its owner.

Generally, an eligible entity that does not file this form will be classified under the default rules described below. An eligible entity that chooses not to be classified under the default rules or that wishes to change its current classification must file Form 8832 to elect a classification. The IRS will use the information entered on this form to establish the entity's filing and reporting requirements for Federal tax purposes.

60-month limitation rule. Once an eligible entity makes an election to change its classification, the entity generally cannot change its classification by election again during the 60 months after the effective date of the election. However, the IRS may (**by private letter ruling**) permit the entity to change its classification by election within the 60-month period if more than 50% of the ownership interests in the entity as of the effective date of the election are owned by persons that did not own any interests in the entity on the effective date of the entity's prior election. See Regulations section 301.7701-3(c)(1)(iv) for more details.

Note: *The 60-month limitation does not apply if the previous election was made by a newly formed eligible entity and was effective on the date of formation.*

Default Rules

Existing entity default rule. Certain domestic and foreign entities that were in existence before January 1, 1997, and have an established Federal tax classification generally do not need to make an election to continue that classification. If an existing entity decides to change its classification, it may do so subject to the 60-month limitation rule. See Regulations sections 301.7701-3(b)(3) and 301.7701-3(h)(2) for more details.

Domestic default rule. Unless an election is made on Form 8832, a domestic eligible entity is:

1. A partnership if it has two or more members.

2. Disregarded as an entity separate from its owner if it has a single owner.

A change in the number of members of an eligible entity classified as an association does not affect the entity's classification. However, an eligible entity classified as a partnership will become a disregarded entity when the entity's membership is reduced to one member and a disregarded entity will be classified as a partnership when the entity has more than one member.

Foreign default rule. Unless an election is made on Form 8832, a foreign eligible entity is:

1. A partnership if it has two or more members and **at least** one member does not have limited liability.

2. An association taxable as a corporation if all members have limited liability.

3. Disregarded as an entity separate from its owner if it has a single owner that does not have limited liability.

Definitions

Association. For purposes of this form, an association is an eligible entity that is taxable as a corporation by election or, for foreign eligible entities, under the default rules (see Regulations section 301.7701-3).

Business entity. A business entity is any entity recognized for Federal tax purposes that is not properly classified as a trust under Regulations section 301.7701-4 or otherwise subject to special

treatment under the Code. See Regulations section 301.7701-2(a).

Corporation. For Federal tax purposes, a corporation is any of the following:

1. A business entity organized under a Federal or state statute, or under a statute of a federally recognized Indian tribe, if the statute describes or refers to the entity as incorporated or as a corporation, body corporate, or body politic.

2. An association (as determined under Regulations section 301.7701-3).

3. A business entity organized under a state statute, if the statute describes or refers to the entity as a joint-stock company or joint-stock association.

4. An insurance company.

5. A state-chartered business entity conducting banking activities, if any of its deposits are insured under the Federal Deposit Insurance Act, as amended, 12 U.S.C. 1811 et seq., or a similar Federal statute.

6. A business entity wholly owned by a state or any political subdivision thereof, or a business entity wholly owned by a foreign government or any other entity described in Regulations section 1.892-2T.

7. A business entity that is taxable as a corporation under a provision of the Code other than section 7701(a)(3).

8. A foreign business entity listed on page 5. See Regulations section 301.7701-2(b)(8) for any exceptions and inclusions to items on this list and for any revisions made to this list since these instructions were printed.

Disregarded entity. A disregarded entity is an eligible entity that is treated as an entity that is not separate from its single owner. Its separate existence will be ignored for Federal tax purposes unless it elects corporate tax treatment.

Eligible entity. An eligible entity is a business entity that is not included in items **1** or **3** through **8** under the definition of corporation above.

Limited liability. A member of a foreign eligible entity has limited liability if the member has no personal liability for any debts of or claims against the entity by reason of being a member. This determination is based solely on the statute or law under which the entity is organized (and, if relevant, the entity's organizational documents). A member has personal liability if the creditors of the entity may seek satisfaction of all or any part of the debts or claims against the entity from the member as such. A member has personal liability even if the member makes an agreement under which another person (whether or not a member of the entity) assumes that liability or agrees to indemnify that member for that liability.

Partnership. A partnership is a business entity that has **at least** two members and is not a corporation as defined on page 2.

Who Must File

File this form for an **eligible entity** that is one of the following:

● A domestic entity electing to be classified as an association taxable as a corporation.

● A domestic entity electing to change its current classification (even if it is currently classified under the default rule).

● A foreign entity that has more than one owner, all owners having limited liability, electing to be classified as a partnership.

● A foreign entity that has at least one owner that does not have limited liability, electing to be classified as an association taxable as a corporation.

● A foreign entity with a single owner having limited liability, electing to be an entity disregarded as an entity separate from its owner.

● A foreign entity electing to change its current classification (even if it is currently classified under the default rule).

   Do not file this form for an eligible entity that is:

● Tax-exempt under section 501(a) or

● A real estate investment trust (REIT), as defined in section 856.

Effect of Election

The Federal tax treatment of elective changes in classification as described in Regulations section 301.7701-3(g)(1) is summarized as follows:

● If an eligible entity classified as a partnership elects to be classified as an association, it is deemed that the

partnership contributes all of its assets and liabilities to the association in exchange for stock in the association, and immediately thereafter, the partnership liquidates by distributing the stock of the association to its partners.

● If an eligible entity classified as an association elects to be classified as a partnership, it is deemed that the association distributes all of its assets and liabilities to its shareholders in liquidation of the association, and immediately thereafter, the shareholders contribute all of the distributed assets and liabilities to a newly formed partnership.

● If an eligible entity classified as an association elects to be disregarded as an entity separate from its owner, it is deemed that the association distributes all of its assets and liabilities to its single owner in liquidation of the association.

● If an eligible entity that is disregarded as an entity separate from its owner elects to be classified as an association, the owner of the eligible entity is deemed to have contributed all of the assets and liabilities of the entity to the association in exchange for the stock of the association.

Note: *For information on the Federal tax treatment of elective changes in classification, see Regulations section 301.7701-3(g).*

When To File

See the instructions for line 4.

A newly formed entity may be eligible for late election relief under Rev. Proc. 2002-59, 2002-39 I.R.B. 615 if:

● The entity failed to obtain its desired classified election solely because Form 8832 was not timely filed,

● The due date for the entity's desired classification tax return (excluding extension) for the tax year beginning with the entity's formation date has not passed, and

● The entity has reasonable cause for its failure to make a timely election.

   To obtain relief, a newly formed entity must file Form 8832 on or before the due date of the first Federal tax return (excluding extensions) of the entity's desired classification. The entity must also

write "FILED PURSUANT TO REV. PROC. 2002-59" at the top of the form. The entity must attach a statement to the form explaining why it failed to file a timely election. If Rev. Proc. 2002-59 does not apply, an entity may seek relief for a late entity election by requesting a private letter ruling and paying a user fee in accordance with Rev. Proc. 2002-1, 2002-1 I.R.B. 1 (or its successor).

Where To File

File Form 8832 with the Internal Revenue Service Center, Philadelphia, PA 19255. Also attach a copy of Form 8832 to the entity's Federal income tax or information return for the tax year of the election. If the entity is not required to file a return for that year, a copy of its Form 8832 **must** be attached to the Federal income tax or information returns of **all** direct or indirect owners of the entity for the tax year of the owner that includes the date on which the election took effect. Although failure to attach a copy will not invalidate an otherwise valid election, each member of the entity is required to file returns that are consistent with the entity's election. In addition, penalties may be assessed against persons who are required to, but who do not, attach Form 8832 to their returns. Other penalties may apply for filing Federal income tax or information returns inconsistent with the entity's election.

Specific Instructions

Name. Enter the name of the eligible entity electing to be classified using Form 8832.

Employer identification number (EIN). Show the correct EIN of the eligible entity electing to be classified. Any entity that has an EIN will retain that EIN even if its Federal tax classification changes under Regulations section 301.7701-3.

   If a disregarded entity's classification changes so that it is recognized as a partnership or association for Federal tax purposes, and that entity had an EIN, then the entity must use that EIN and not the identifying number of the single owner. If the entity did not already have its own EIN, then the entity must apply for an EIN and not use the identifying number of the single owner.

220

A foreign person that makes an election under Regulations section 301.7701-3(c) must also use its own taxpayer identifying number. See sections 6721 through 6724 for penalties that may apply for failure to supply taxpayer identifying numbers.

If the entity electing to be classified using Form 8832 does not have an EIN, it must apply for one on **Form SS-4,** Application for Employer Identification Number. If the filing of Form 8832 is the only reason the entity is applying for an EIN, check the "Other" box on line 9 of Form SS-4 and write "Form 8832" to the right of that box. If the entity has not received an EIN by the time Form 8832 is due, write "Applied for" in the space for the EIN. **Do not** apply for a new EIN for an existing entity that is changing its classification if the entity already has an EIN.

Address. Enter the address of the entity electing a classification. Include the suite, room, or other unit number after the street address. If the Post Office does not deliver mail to the street address and the entity has a P.O. box, show the box number instead of the street address.

Line 1. Check box 1a if the entity is choosing a classification for the first time **and** the entity does not want to be classified under the applicable default classification. **Do not** file this form if the entity wants to be classified under the default rules.

Check box 1b if the entity is changing its current classification.

Line 2. Check the appropriate box if you are changing a current classification (no matter how achieved), or are electing out of a default classification. **Do not** file this form if you fall within a default classification that is the desired classification for the new entity.

Line 3. If an eligible entity has checked box 2c or box 2f and is electing to be disregarded as an entity separate from its owner, it must enter the name of its owner on line 3a and the owner's identifying number (social security number, or individual taxpayer identification number, or EIN) on line 3b. If the owner is a foreign person or entity and does not have a U.S. identifying number, enter "none" on line 3b. If the entity making the election is foreign, enter the name of the country in which it was formed on line 3c.

Line 4. Generally, the election will take effect on the date you enter on line 4 of this form or on the date filed if no date is entered on line 4. However, an election specifying an entity's classification for Federal tax purposes can take effect no more than 75 days prior to the date the election is filed, nor can it take effect later than 12 months after the date on which the election is filed. If line 4 shows a date more than 75 days prior to the date on which the election is filed, the election will take effect 75 days before the date it is filed. If line 4 shows an effective date more than 12 months from the filing date, the election will take effect 12 months after the date the election was filed.

Consent statement and signatures. Form 8832 must be signed by:

1. Each member of the electing entity who is an owner at the time the election is filed; or

2. Any officer, manager, or member of the electing entity who is authorized (under local law or the organizational documents) to make the election and who represents to having such authorization under penalties of perjury.

If an election is to be effective for any period prior to the time it is filed, each person who was an owner between the date the election is to be effective and the date the election is filed, and who is not an owner at the time the election is filed, must also sign.

If you need a continuation sheet or use a separate consent statement, attach it to Form 8832. The separate consent statement must contain the same information as shown on Form 8832.

Paperwork Reduction Act Notice

We ask for the information on this form to carry out the Internal Revenue laws of the United States. You are required to give us the information. We need it to ensure that you are complying with these laws and to allow us to figure and collect the right amount of tax.

You are not required to provide the information requested on a form that is subject to the Paperwork Reduction Act unless the form displays a valid OMB control number. Books or records relating to a form or its instructions must be retained as long as their contents may become material in the administration of any Internal Revenue law. Generally, tax returns and return information are confidential, as required by section 6103.

The time needed to complete and file this form will vary depending on individual circumstances. The estimated average time is:

Recordkeeping . . . 1 hr., 49 min.

Learning about the law or the form . . . 2 hr.,   7 min.

Preparing and sending the form to the IRS . . . . 23 min.

If you have comments concerning the accuracy of these time estimates or suggestions for making this form simpler, we would be happy to hear from you. You can write to the Tax Forms Committee, Western Area Distribution Center, Rancho Cordova, CA 95743-0001. **Do not** send the form to this address. Instead, see **Where To File** on page 3.

Foreign Entities Classified as Corporations for Federal Tax Purposes:

American Samoa- Corporation
Argentina- Sociedad Anonima
Australia- Public Limited Company
Austria- Aktiengesellschaft
Barbados- Limited Company
Belgium- Societe Anonyme
Belize- Public Limited Company
Bolivia- Sociedad Anonima
Brazil- Sociedade Anonima
Canada- Corporation and Company
Chile- Sociedad Anonima
People's Republic of China- Gufen Youxian Gongsi
Republic of China (Taiwan)- Ku-fen Yu-hsien Kung-szu
Colombia- Sociedad Anonima
Costa Rica- Sociedad Anonima
Cyprus- Public Limited Company
Czech Republic- Akciova Spolecnost
Denmark- Aktieselskab
Ecuador- Sociedad Anonima or Compania Anonima
Egypt- Sharikat Al-Mossahamah
El Salvador- Sociedad Anonima
Finland- Julkinen Osakeyhtio/ Publikt Aktiebolag
France- Societe Anonyme
Germany- Aktiengesellschaft
Greece- Anonymos Etairia
Guam- Corporation
Guatemala- Sociedad Anonima
Guyana- Public Limited Company
Honduras- Sociedad Anonima
Hong Kong- Public Limited Company
Hungary- Reszvenytarsasag

Iceland- Hlutafelag
India- Public Limited Company
Indonesia- Perseroan Terbuka
Ireland- Public Limited Company
Israel- Public Limited Company
Italy- Societa per Azioni
Jamaica- Public Limited Company
Japan- Kabushiki Kaisha
Kazakstan- Ashyk Aktsionerlik Kogham
Republic of Korea- Chusik Hoesa
Liberia- Corporation
Luxembourg- Societe Anonyme
Malaysia- Berhad
Malta- Public Limited Company
Mexico- Sociedad Anonima
Morocco- Societe Anonyme
Netherlands- Naamloze Vennootschap
New Zealand- Limited Company
Nicaragua- Compania Anonima
Nigeria- Public Limited Company
Northern Mariana Islands- Corporation
Norway- Allment Aksjeselskap
Pakistan- Public Limited Company
Panama- Sociedad Anonima
Paraguay- Sociedad Anonima
Peru- Sociedad Anonima
Philippines- Stock Corporation
Poland- Spolka Akcyjna
Portugal- Sociedade Anonima
Puerto Rico- Corporation
Romania- Societe pe Actiuni
Russia- Otkrytoye Aktsionernoy Obshchestvo

Saudi Arabia- Sharikat Al-Mossahamah
Singapore- Public Limited Company
Slovak Republic- Akciova Spolocnost
South Africa- Public Limited Company
Spain- Sociedad Anonima
Surinam- Naamloze Vennootschap
Sweden- Publika Aktiebolag
Switzerland- Aktiengesellschaft
Thailand- Borisat Chamkad (Mahachon)
Trinidad and Tobago- Limited Company
Tunisia- Societe Anonyme
Turkey- Anonim Sirket
Ukraine- Aktsionerne Tovaristvo Vidkritogo Tipu
United Kingdom- Public Limited Company
United States Virgin Islands- Corporation
Uruguay- Sociedad Anonima
Venezuela- Sociedad Anonima or Compania Anonima

⚠ **CAUTION**

See Regulations section 301.7701-2(b)(8) for any exceptions and inclusions to items on this list and for any revisions made to this list since these instructions were printed.

This page intentionally left blank.

Form **2553**
(Rev. December 2002)

Department of the Treasury
Internal Revenue Service

Election by a Small Business Corporation

(Under section 1362 of the Internal Revenue Code)

▶ See Parts II and III on back and the separate instructions.

▶ **The corporation may either send or fax this form to the IRS. See page 2 of the instructions.**

OMB No. 1545-0146

Notes: 1. *Do not* file **Form 1120S,** U.S. Income Tax Return for an S Corporation, for any tax year before the year the election takes effect.

2. This election to be an S corporation can be accepted only if all the tests are met under **Who May Elect** on page 1 of the instructions; all shareholders have signed the consent statement; and the exact name and address of the corporation and other required form information are provided.

3. If the corporation was in existence before the effective date of this election, see **Taxes an S Corporation May Owe** on page 1 of the instructions.

Part I   Election Information

Please Type or Print

Name of corporation (see instructions)	**A** Employer identification number
Number, street, and room or suite no. (If a P.O. box, see instructions.)	**B** Date incorporated
City or town, state, and ZIP code	**C** State of incorporation

D Check the applicable box(es) if the corporation, after applying for the EIN shown in **A** above, changed its name ☐ or address ☐

E Election is to be effective for tax year beginning (month, day, year) . . . . ▶ / /

F Name and title of officer or legal representative who the IRS may call for more information

G Telephone number of officer or legal representative

(   )

H If this election takes effect for the first tax year the corporation exists, enter month, day, and year of the **earliest** of the following: (1) date the corporation first had shareholders, (2) date the corporation first had assets, or (3) date the corporation began doing business . . . . ▶ / /

I Selected tax year: Annual return will be filed for tax year ending (month and day) ▶ -

If the tax year ends on any date other than December 31, except for a 52–53-week tax year ending with reference to the month of December, you **must** complete Part II on the back. If the date you enter is the ending date of a 52–53-week tax year, write "52–53-week year" to the right of the date.

J Name and address of each shareholder; shareholder's spouse having a community property interest in the corporation's stock; and each tenant in common, joint tenant, and tenant by the entirety. (A husband and wife (and their estates) are counted as one shareholder in determining the number of shareholders without regard to the manner in which the stock is owned.)	**K** Shareholders' Consent Statement. Under penalties of perjury, we declare that we consent to the election of the above-named corporation to be an S corporation under section 1362(a) and that we have examined this consent statement, including accompanying schedules and statements, and to the best of our knowledge and belief, it is true, correct, and complete. We understand our consent is binding and may not be withdrawn after the corporation has made a valid election. (Shareholders sign and date below.)		**L** Stock owned		**M** Social security number or employer identification number (see instructions)	**N** Shareholder's tax year ends (month and day)
	Signature	Date	Number of shares	Dates acquired		

Under penalties of perjury, I declare that I have examined this election, including accompanying schedules and statements, and to the best of my knowledge and belief, it is true, correct, and complete.

Signature of officer ▶   Title ▶   Date ▶

For Paperwork Reduction Act Notice, see page 4 of the instructions.   Cat. No. 18629R   Form **2553** (Rev. 12-2002)

224

Part II   **Selection of Fiscal Tax Year** (All corporations using this part must complete item O and item P, Q, or R.)

O   Check the applicable box to indicate whether the corporation is:

    1. ☐ A new corporation adopting the tax year entered in item I, Part I.

    2. ☐ An existing corporation retaining the tax year entered in item I, Part I.

    3. ☐ An existing corporation changing to the tax year entered in item I, Part I.

P   Complete item P if the corporation is using the automatic approval provisions of Rev. Proc. 2002-38, 2002-22 I.R.B. 1037, to request **(1)** a natural business year (as defined in section 5.05 of Rev. Proc. 2002-38) or **(2)** a year that satisfies the ownership tax year test (as defined in section 5.06 of Rev. Proc. 2002-38). Check the applicable box below to indicate the representation statement the corporation is making.

    1. Natural Business Year ▶ ☐ I represent that the corporation is adopting, retaining, or changing to a tax year that qualifies as its natural business year as defined in section 5.05 of Rev. Proc. 2002-38 and has attached a statement verifying that it satisfies the 25% gross receipts test (see instructions for content of statement). I also represent that the corporation is not precluded by section 4.02 of Rev. Proc. 2002-38 from obtaining automatic approval of such adoption, retention, or change in tax year.

    2. Ownership Tax Year ▶ ☐ I represent that shareholders (as described in section 5.06 of Rev. Proc. 2002-38) holding more than half of the shares of the stock (as of the first day of the tax year to which the request relates) of the corporation have the same tax year or are concurrently changing to the tax year that the corporation adopts, retains, or changes to per item I, Part I, and that such tax year satisfies the requirement of section 4.01(3) of Rev. Proc. 2002-38. I also represent that the corporation is not precluded by section 4.02 of Rev. Proc. 2002-38 from obtaining automatic approval of such adoption, retention, or change in tax year.

Note: *If you do not use item P and the corporation wants a fiscal tax year, complete either item Q or R below. Item Q is used to request a fiscal tax year based on a business purpose and to make a back-up section 444 election. Item R is used to make a regular section 444 election.*

Q   Business Purpose- To request a fiscal tax year based on a business purpose, you must check box Q1. See instructions for details including payment of a user fee. You may also check box Q2 and/or box Q3.

    1. Check here ▶ ☐ if the fiscal year entered in item I, Part I, is requested under the prior approval provisions of Rev. Proc. 2002-39, 2002-22 I.R.B. 1046. Attach to Form 2553 a statement describing the relevant facts and circumstances and, if applicable, the gross receipts from sales and services necessary to establish a business purpose. See the instructions for details regarding the gross receipts from sales and services. If the IRS proposes to disapprove the requested fiscal year, do you want a conference with the IRS National Office?
    ☐ Yes   ☐ No

    2. Check here ▶ ☐ to show that the corporation intends to make a back-up section 444 election in the event the corporation's business purpose request is not approved by the IRS. (See instructions for more information.)

    3. Check here ▶ ☐ to show that the corporation agrees to adopt or change to a tax year ending December 31 if necessary for the IRS to accept this election for S corporation status in the event (1) the corporation's business purpose request is not approved and the corporation makes a back-up section 444 election, but is ultimately not qualified to make a section 444 election, or (2) the corporation's business purpose request is not approved and the corporation did not make a back-up section 444 election.

R   Section 444 Election- To make a section 444 election, you must check box R1 and you may also check box R2.

    1. Check here ▶ ☐ to show the corporation will make, if qualified, a section 444 election to have the fiscal tax year shown in item I, Part I. To make the election, you must complete **Form 8716,** Election To Have a Tax Year Other Than a Required Tax Year, and either attach it to Form 2553 or file it separately.

    2. Check here ▶ ☐ to show that the corporation agrees to adopt or change to a tax year ending December 31 if necessary for the IRS to accept this election for S corporation status in the event the corporation is ultimately not qualified to make a section 444 election.

Part III   **Qualified Subchapter S Trust (QSST) Election Under Section 1361(d)(2)***

Income beneficiary's name and address	Social security number
Trust's name and address	Employer identification number

Date on which stock of the corporation was transferred to the trust (month, day, year) . . . . ▶   /   /

In order for the trust named above to be a QSST and thus a qualifying shareholder of the S corporation for which this Form 2553 is filed, I hereby make the election under section 1361(d)(2). Under penalties of perjury, I certify that the trust meets the definitional requirements of section 1361(d)(3) and that all other information provided in Part III is true, correct, and complete.

_____   _____

Signature of income beneficiary or signature and title of legal representative or other qualified person making the election   Date

*Use Part III to make the QSST election only if stock of the corporation has been transferred to the trust on or before the date on which the corporation makes its election to be an S corporation. The QSST election must be made and filed separately if stock of the corporation is transferred to the trust after the date on which the corporation makes the S election.

Instructions for Form 2553

(Rev. December 2002)

Election by a Small Business Corporation

Section references are to the Internal Revenue Code unless otherwise noted.

Department of the Treasury
Internal Revenue Service

General Instructions

Purpose

To elect to be an S corporation, a corporation must file Form 2553. The election permits the income of the S corporation to be taxed to the shareholders of the corporation rather than to the corporation itself, except as noted below under **Taxes an S Corporation May Owe.**

Who May Elect

A corporation may elect to be an S corporation only if it meets all of the following tests:

1. It is a domestic corporation.

Note: *A limited liability company (LLC)* **must** *file* **Form 8832**, *Entity Classification Election, to elect to be treated as an association taxable as a corporation in order to elect to be an S corporation.*

2. It has no more than 75 shareholders. A husband and wife (and their estates) are treated as one shareholder for this requirement. All other persons are treated as separate shareholders.

3. Its only shareholders are individuals, estates, exempt organizations described in section 401(a) or 501(c)(3), or certain trusts described in section 1361(c)(2)(A). See the instructions for Part III regarding qualified subchapter S trusts (QSSTs).

A trustee of a trust wanting to make an election under section 1361(e)(3) to be an electing small business trust (ESBT) should see Notice 97-12, 1997-1 C.B. 385. However, in general, for tax years beginning after May 13, 2002, Notice 97-12 is superseded by Regulations section 1.1361-1(c)(1). Also see Rev. Proc. 98-23, 1998-1 C.B. 662, for guidance on how to convert a QSST to an ESBT. However, in general, for tax years beginning after May 13, 2002, Rev. Proc. 98-23 is superseded by Regulations section 1.1361-1(j)(12). If there was an inadvertent failure to timely file an ESBT election, see the relief provisions under Rev. Proc. 98-55, 1998-2 C.B. 643.

4. It has no nonresident alien shareholders.

5. It has only one class of stock (disregarding differences in voting rights). Generally, a corporation is treated as having only one class of stock if all outstanding shares of the corporation's stock confer identical rights to distribution and liquidation proceeds. See Regulations section 1.1361-1(l) for details.

6. It is not one of the following ineligible corporations:

a. A bank or thrift institution that uses the reserve method of accounting for bad debts under section 585,

b. An insurance company subject to tax under the rules of subchapter L of the Code,

c. A corporation that has elected to be treated as a possessions corporation under section 936, or

d. A domestic international sales corporation (DISC) or former DISC.

7. It has a permitted tax year as required by section 1378 or makes a section 444 election to have a tax year other than a permitted tax year. Section 1378 defines a permitted tax year as a tax year ending December 31, or any other tax year for which the corporation establishes a business purpose to the satisfaction of the IRS. See Part II for details on requesting a fiscal tax year based on a business purpose or on making a section 444 election.

8. Each shareholder consents as explained in the instructions for column K.

See sections 1361, 1362, and 1378 for additional information on the above tests.

A parent S corporation can elect to treat an eligible wholly-owned subsidiary as a qualified subchapter S subsidiary (QSub). If the election is made, the assets, liabilities, and items of income, deduction, and credit of the QSub are treated as those of the parent. To make the election, get **Form 8869,** Qualified Subchapter S Subsidiary Election. If the QSub election was not timely filed, the corporation may be entitled to relief under Rev. Proc. 98-55.

Taxes an S Corporation May Owe

An S corporation may owe income tax in the following instances:

1. If, at the end of any tax year, the corporation had accumulated earnings and profits, and its passive investment income under section 1362(d)(3) is more than 25% of its gross receipts, the corporation may owe tax on its excess net passive income.

2. A corporation with net recognized built-in gain (as defined in section 1374(d)(2)) may owe tax on its built-in gains.

3. A corporation that claimed investment credit before its first year as an S corporation will be liable for any investment credit recapture tax.

4. A corporation that used the LIFO inventory method for the year immediately preceding its first year as an S corporation may owe an additional tax due to LIFO recapture. The tax is paid in four equal installments, the first of which must be paid by the due date (not including extensions) of the corporation's income tax return for its last tax year as a C corporation.

For more details on these taxes, see the Instructions for Form 1120S.

Where To File

Send the original election (no photocopies) or fax it to the Internal Revenue Service Center listed below. If the corporation files this election by fax, keep the original Form 2553 with the corporation's permanent records.

If the corporation's principal business, office, or agency is located in ▼	Use the following Internal Revenue Service Center address or fax number ▼
Connecticut, Delaware, District of Columbia, Illinois, Indiana, Kentucky, Maine, Maryland, Massachusetts, Michigan, New Hampshire, New Jersey, New York, North Carolina, Ohio, Pennsylvania, Rhode Island, South Carolina, Vermont, Virginia, West Virginia, Wisconsin	Cincinnati, OH 45999 (859) 669-5748
Alabama, Alaska, Arizona, Arkansas, California, Colorado, Florida, Georgia, Hawaii, Idaho, Iowa, Kansas, Louisiana, Minnesota, Mississippi, Missouri, Montana, Nebraska, Nevada, New Mexico, North Dakota, Oklahoma, Oregon, South Dakota, Tennessee, Texas, Utah, Washington, Wyoming	Ogden, UT 84201 (801) 620-7116

When To Make the Election

Complete and file Form 2553 **(a)** at any time before the 16th day of the 3rd month of the tax year, if filed during the tax year the election is to take effect, or **(b)** at any time during the preceding tax year. An election made no later than 2 months and 15 days after the beginning of a tax year that is less than 2½ months long is treated as timely made for that tax year. **An election made after the 15th day of the 3rd month but before the end of the tax year is effective for the next year.** For example, if a calendar tax year corporation makes the election in April 2002, it is effective for the corporation's 2003 calendar tax year.

However, an election made after the due date will be accepted as timely filed if the corporation can show that the failure to file on time was due to reasonable cause. To request relief for a late election, the corporation generally must request a private letter ruling and pay a user fee in accordance with Rev. Proc. 2002-1, 2002-1 I.R.B. 1 (or its successor). But if the election is filed within 12 months of its due date and the original due date for filing the corporation's initial Form 1120S has not passed, the ruling and user fee requirements do not apply. To

request relief in this case, write "FILED PURSUANT TO REV. PROC. 98-55" at the top of page 1 of Form 2553, attach a statement explaining the reason for failing to file the election on time, and file Form 2553 as otherwise instructed. See Rev. Proc. 98-55 for more details.

See Regulations section 1.1362-6(b)(3)(iii) for how to obtain relief for an inadvertent invalid election if the corporation filed a timely election, but one or more shareholders did not file a timely consent.

Acceptance or Nonacceptance of Election

The service center will notify the corporation if its election is accepted and when it will take effect. The corporation will also be notified if its election is not accepted. The corporation should generally receive a determination on its election within 60 days after it has filed Form 2553. If box Q1 in Part II is checked on page 2, the corporation will receive a ruling letter from the IRS in Washington, DC, that either approves or denies the selected tax year. When box Q1 is checked, it will generally take an additional 90 days for the Form 2553 to be accepted.

Care should be exercised to ensure that the IRS receives the election. If the corporation is not notified of acceptance or nonacceptance of its election within 3 months of the date of filing (date mailed), or within 6 months if box Q1 is checked, take follow-up action by corresponding with the service center where the corporation filed the election.

If the IRS questions whether Form 2553 was filed, an acceptable proof of filing is **(a)** certified or registered mail receipt (timely postmarked) from the U.S. Postal Service, or its equivalent from a designated private delivery service (see Notice 2002-62, 2002-39 I.R.B. 574 (or its successor)); **(b)** Form 2553 with accepted stamp; **(c)** Form 2553 with stamped IRS received date; or **(d)** IRS letter stating that Form 2553 has been accepted.

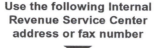 *Do not file Form 1120S for any tax year before the year the election takes effect. If the corporation is now required to file **Form 1120,** U.S. Corporation Income Tax Return, or any other applicable tax return, continue filing it until the election takes effect.*

End of Election

Once the election is made, it stays in effect until it is terminated. If the election is terminated in a tax year beginning after 1996, IRS consent is generally required for another election by the corporation (or a successor corporation) on Form 2553 for any tax year before the 5th tax year after the first tax year in which the termination took effect. See Regulations section 1.1362-5 for details.

Specific Instructions

Part I (*All corporations must complete.*)

Name and Address of Corporation

Enter the true corporate name as stated in the corporate charter or other legal document creating it. If the corporation's mailing address is the same as someone else's, such as a shareholder's, enter "c/o" and this person's name following the name of the corporation. Include the suite, room, or other unit number after the street address. If the Post Office does not deliver to the street address and the corporation has a P.O. box, show the box number instead of the street address. If the corporation changed its name or address after applying for its employer identification number, be sure to check the box in item D of Part I.

Item A. Employer Identification Number (EIN)

If the corporation has applied for an EIN but has not received it, enter "applied for." If the corporation does not have an EIN, it should apply for one on **Form SS-4,** Application for Employer Identification Number. You can order Form SS-4 by calling 1-800-TAX-FORM (1-800-829-3676) or by accessing the IRS Web Site **www.irs.gov**.

Item E. Effective Date of Election

Enter the beginning effective date (month, day, year) of the tax year requested for the S corporation. Generally, this will be the beginning date of the tax year for which the ending effective date is required to be shown in item I, Part I. For a new corporation (first year the corporation exists) it will generally be the date required to be shown in item H, Part I. The tax year of a new corporation starts on the date that it has shareholders, acquires assets, or begins doing business, whichever happens first. If the effective date for item E for a newly formed corporation is later than the date in item H, the corporation should file Form 1120 or Form 1120-A for the tax period between these dates.

Column K. Shareholders' Consent Statement

Each shareholder who owns (or is deemed to own) stock at the time the election is made must consent to the election. If the election is made during the corporation's tax year for which it first takes effect, any person who held stock at any time during the part of that year that occurs before the election is made, must consent to the election, even though the person may have sold or transferred his or her stock before the election is made.

An election made during the first 2½ months of the tax year is effective for the following tax year if any person who held stock in the corporation during the part of the tax year before the election was made, and who did not hold stock at the time the election was made, did not consent to the election.

Note: *Once the election is made, a new shareholder is not required to consent to the election; a new Form 2553 will not be required.*

Each shareholder consents by signing and dating in column K or signing and dating a separate consent statement described below. The following special rules apply in determining who must sign the consent statement.
- If a husband and wife have a community interest in the stock or in the income from it, both must consent.
- Each tenant in common, joint tenant, and tenant by the entirety must consent.
- A minor's consent is made by the minor, legal representative of the minor, or a natural or adoptive parent of the minor if no legal representative has been appointed.
- The consent of an estate is made by the executor or administrator.
- The consent of an electing small business trust is made by the trustee.
- If the stock is owned by a trust (other than an electing small business trust), the deemed owner of the trust must consent. See section 1361(c)(2) for details regarding trusts that are permitted to be shareholders and rules for determining who is the deemed owner.

Continuation sheet or separate consent statement. If you need a continuation sheet or use a separate consent statement, attach it to Form 2553. The separate consent statement must contain the name, address, and EIN of the corporation and the shareholder information requested in columns J through N of Part I. If you want, you may combine all the shareholders' consents in one statement.

Column L

Enter the number of shares of stock each shareholder owns and the dates the stock was acquired. If the election is made during the corporation's tax year for which it first takes effect, do not list the shares of stock for those shareholders who sold or transferred all of their stock before the election was made. However, these shareholders must still consent to the election for it to be effective for the tax year.

Column M

Enter the social security number of each shareholder who is an individual. Enter the EIN of each shareholder that is an estate, a qualified trust, or an exempt organization.

Column N

Enter the month and day that each shareholder's tax year ends. If a shareholder is changing his or her tax year, enter the tax year the shareholder is changing to, and attach an explanation indicating the present tax year and the basis for the change (e.g., automatic revenue procedure or letter ruling request).

Signature

Form 2553 must be signed by the president, treasurer, assistant treasurer, chief accounting officer, or other corporate officer (such as tax officer) authorized to sign.

Part II

Complete Part II if you selected a tax year ending on any date other than December 31 (other than a 52-53-week tax year ending with reference to the month of December).

Note: *In certain circumstances the corporation may not obtain automatic approval of a fiscal year under the natural business year (Box P1) or ownership tax year (Box P2) provisions if it is under examination, before an area office, or before a federal court with respect to any income tax issue and the annual accounting period is under consideration. For details, see section 4.02 of Rev. Proc. 2002-38, 2002-22 I.R.B. 1037.*

Box P1

Attach a statement showing separately for each month the amount of gross receipts for the most recent 47 months. A corporation that does not have a 47-month period of gross receipts cannot automatically establish a natural business year.

Box Q1

For examples of an acceptable business purpose for requesting a fiscal tax year, see section 5.02 of Rev. Proc. 2002-39, 2002-22 I.R.B. 1046, and Rev. Rul. 87-57, 1987-2 C.B. 117.

Attach a statement showing the relevant facts and circumstances to establish a business purpose for the requested fiscal year. For details on what is sufficient to establish a business purpose, see section 5.02 of Rev. Proc. 2002-39.

If your business purpose is based on one of the natural business year tests provided in section 5.03 of Rev. Proc. 2002-39, identify if you are using the 25% gross receipts, annual business cycle, or seasonal business test. For the 25% gross receipts test, provide a schedule showing the amount of gross receipts for each month for the most recent 47 months. For either the annual business cycle or seasonal business test, provide the gross receipts from sales and services (and inventory costs, if applicable) for each month of the short period, if any, and the three immediately preceding tax years. If the corporation has been in existence for less than three tax years, submit figures for the period of existence.

If you check box Q1, you will be charged a user fee of up to $600 (subject to change—see Rev. Proc. 2002-1 or its successor). Do not pay the fee when filing Form 2553. The service center will send Form 2553 to the IRS in Washington, DC, who, in turn, will notify the corporation that the fee is due.

Box Q2

If the corporation makes a back-up section 444 election for which it is qualified, then the election will take effect in the event the business purpose request is not approved. In some cases, the tax year requested under the back-up section 444 election may be different than the tax year requested under business purpose. See **Form 8716,** Election To Have a Tax Year Other Than a Required Tax Year, for details on making a back-up section 444 election.

Boxes Q2 and R2

If the corporation is not qualified to make the section 444 election after making the item Q2 back-up section 444 election or indicating its intention to make the election in item R1, and therefore it later files a calendar year return, it should write "Section 444 Election Not Made" in the top left corner of the first calendar year Form 1120S it files.

Part III

Certain qualified subchapter S trusts (QSSTs) may make the QSST election required by section 1361(d)(2) in Part III. Part III may be used to make the QSST election only if corporate stock has been transferred to the trust on or before the date on which the corporation makes its election to be an S corporation. However, a statement can be used instead of Part III to make the election. If there was an inadvertent failure to timely file a QSST election, see the relief provisions under Rev. Proc. 98-55.

Note: *Use Part III only if you make the election in Part I (i.e., Form 2553 cannot be filed with only Part III completed).*

The deemed owner of the QSST must also consent to the S corporation election in column K, page 1, of Form 2553. See section 1361(c)(2).

Paperwork Reduction Act Notice. We ask for the information on this form to carry out the Internal Revenue laws of the United States. You are required to give us the information. We need it to ensure that you are complying with these laws and to allow us to figure and collect the right amount of tax.

You are not required to provide the information requested on a form that is subject to the Paperwork Reduction Act unless the form displays a valid OMB control number. Books or records relating to a form or its instructions must be retained as long as their contents may become material in the administration of any Internal Revenue law. Generally, tax returns and return information are confidential, as required by section 6103.

The time needed to complete and file this form will depend on individual circumstances. The estimated average time is:

Recordkeeping	9 hr., 34 min.
Learning about the law or the form	3 hr., 28 min.
Preparing, copying, assembling, and sending the form to the IRS	3 hr., 47 min.

If you have comments concerning the accuracy of these time estimates or suggestions for making this form simpler, we would be happy to hear from you. You can write to the Tax Forms Committee, Western Area Distribution Center, Rancho Cordova, CA 95743-0001. **Do not** send the form to this address. Instead, see **Where To File** on page 2.

BILL OF SALE

The undersigned, in consideration of membership interest in _____

_____, a _____ limited liability company, hereby grants, bar-

gains, sells, transfers, and delivers unto said corporation the following goods and chattels:

To have and to hold the same forever.

And the undersigned, their heirs, successors, and administrators, covenant and warrant that they are the lawful

owners of the said goods and chattels and that they are free from all encumbrances. That the undersigned have the

right to sell this property and that they will warrant and defend the sale of said property against the lawful claims

and demands of all persons.

IN WITNESS whereof the undersigned have executed this Bill of Sale this ____ day of _____,

_____.

_____

_____

_____

This page intentionally left blank.

LIMITED LIABILITY COMPANY
MEMBER-MANAGED OPERATING AGREEMENT OF

_____

THIS AGREEMENT is made effective as of _____, _____ among the member(s) and the company.

1. Formation. A limited liability company of the above name has been formed under the laws of the state of _____ by filing articles of organization with the secretary of state. The purpose of the business shall be to carry on any activity which is lawful under the jurisdiction in which it operates. The company may operate under a fictitious name or names as long as the company is in compliance with applicable fictitious name registration laws. The term of the company shall be perpetual or until dissolved as provided by law or by vote of the member(s) as provided in this agreement. Upon dissolution the remaining members shall have the power to continue the operation of the company as long as necessary and allowable under state law until the winding up of the affairs of the business has been completed.

2. Members. The initial member(s) shall be listed on Schedule A, which shall accompany and be made a part of this agreement. Additional members may be admitted to membership upon the unanimous consent of the current members. Transfer or pledge of a member's interest may not be made except upon consent of all members.

3. Contributions. The initial capital contribution(s) shall be listed on Schedule A. No member shall be obligated to contribute any more than the amount set forth on Schedule A unless agreed to in writing by all of the members and no member shall have any personal liability for any debt, obligation or liability of the company other than for full payment of his or her capital contribution. No member shall be entitled to interest on the capital contribution. Member voting rights shall be in proportion to the amount of their contributions.

4. Profit and Loss. The profits and losses of the business, and all other taxable or deductible items shall be allocated to the members according to the percentages on Schedule A. Distributions of profits can be made to the member(s) at any time and in any amount, except where prohibited by law.

5. Distributions. The company shall have the power to make distributions to its members in such amounts and at such intervals as a majority of the members deem appropriate according to law.

6. Management. The limited liability company shall be managed by its members listed on Schedule A, which shall accompany and be made a part of this agreement. Any member may bind the company in all matters in the ordinary course of company business. In the event of a dispute between members, final determination shall be made with a vote by the members, votes being proportioned according to capital contributions.

7. Registered Agent. The company shall at all times have a registered agent and registered office. The initial registered agent and registered office shall be listed on Schedule A.

8. Assets. The assets of the company shall be registered in the legal name of the company and not in the names of the individual members.

9. Records and Accounting. The company shall keep an accurate accounting of its affairs using any method of accounting allowed by law. All members shall have a right to inspect the records during normal business hours. The members shall have the power to hire such accountants as they deem necessary or desirable.

10. Banking. The members of the company shall be authorized to set up bank accounts as in their sole discretion are deemed necessary and are authorized to execute any banking resolutions provided by the institution in which the accounts are being set up.

11. Taxes. The company shall file such tax returns as required by law. The company shall elect to be taxed as a majority of the members decide is in their best interests. The "tax matters partner," as required by the Internal Revenue Code, shall be listed on Schedule A.

12. Separate Entity. The company is a legal entity separate from its members. No member shall have any separate liability for any debts, obligations, or liability of the company except as provided in this agreement.

13. Indemnity and Exculpation. The limited liability company shall indemnify and hold harmless its members, managers, employees, and agents to the fullest extent allowed by law for acts or omissions done as part of their duties to or for the company. Indemnification shall include all liabilities, expenses, attorney and accountant fees, and other costs reasonably expended. No member shall be liable to the company for acts done in good faith.

14. Meetings. The members shall have no obligation to hold annual or any other meeting, but may hold such meetings if they deem them necessary or desirable.

15. Amendment of this Agreement. This agreement may not be amended except in writing signed by all of the members.

16. Conflict of Interest. No member shall be involved with any business or undertaking which competes with the interests of the company except upon agreement in writing by all of the members.

17. Deadlock. In the event that the members cannot come to an agreement on any matter the members agree to submit the issue to mediation to be paid for by the company. In the event the mediation is unsuccessful, they agree to seek arbitration under the rules of the American Arbitration Association.

18. Dissociation of a Member. A member shall have the right to discontinue membership upon giving thirty days notice. A member shall cease to have the right to membership upon death, court-ordered incapacity, bankruptcy or expulsion. The company shall have the right to buy the interest of any dissociated member at fair market value.

19. Dissolution. The company shall dissolve upon the unanimous consent of all the members or upon any event requiring dissolution under state law. In the event of the death, bankruptcy, permanent incapacity, or withdrawal of a member the remaining members may elect to dissolve or to continue the operation of the company.

20. General Provisions. This agreement is intended to represent the entire agreement between the parties. In the event that any party of this agreement is held to be contrary to law or unenforceable, said party shall be considered amended to comply with the law and such holding shall not affect the enforceability of other terms of this agreement. This agreement shall be binding upon the heirs, successors, and assigns of the members.

21. Miscellaneous. _____

_____

_____

_____

_____

_____

IN WITNESS whereof, the members of the limited liability company sign this agreement and adopt it as their operating agreement this _____ **day of** _____, _____ **.**

_____   _____

_____   _____

_____   _____

LIMITED LIABILITY COMPANY
MANAGEMENT OPERATING AGREEMENT OF

_____

THIS AGREEMENT is made effective as of _____, _____ among the member(s) and the company.

1. Formation. A limited liability company of the above name has been formed under the laws of the state of _____ by filing articles of organization with the secretary of state. The purpose of the business shall be to carry on any activity which is lawful under the jurisdiction in which it operates. The company may operate under a fictitious name or names as long as the company is in compliance with applicable fictitious name registration laws. The term of the company shall be perpetual or until dissolved as provided by law or by vote of the member(s) as provided in this agreement. Upon dissolution the remaining members shall have the power to continue the operation of the company as long as necessary and allowable under state law until the winding up of the affairs of the business has been completed.

2. Members. The initial member(s) shall be listed on Schedule A, which shall accompany and be made a part of this agreement. Additional members may be admitted to membership upon the unanimous consent of the current members. Transfer or pledge of a member's interest may not be made except upon consent of all members.

3. Contributions. The initial capital contribution(s) shall be listed on Schedule A. No member shall be obligated to contribute any more than the amount set forth on Schedule A unless agreed to in writing by all of the members. No member shall have any personal liability for any debt, obligation, or liability of the company other than for full payment of his or her capital contribution. No member shall be entitled to interest on the capital contribution. Member voting rights shall be in proportion to the amount of their contributions.

4. Profit and Loss. The profits and losses of the business, and all other taxable or deductible items shall be allocated to the members according to the percentages on Schedule A. Distributions of profits can be made to the member(s) at any time and in any amount, except where prohibited by law.

5. Distributions. The company shall have the power to make distributions to its members in such amounts and at such intervals as a majority of the members deem appropriate according to law.

6. Management. The limited liability company shall be managed by the managers listed on Schedule A. Any manager may bind the company in all matters in the ordinary course of company business. These managers may or may not be members of the company and each manager shall have an equal vote with other managers as to management decisions. Managers shall serve until resignation or death or until they are removed by a majority vote of the members. Replacement managers shall be selected by a majority vote of the members. Managers shall have no personal liability for expenses, obligations or liabilities of the company.

7. Registered Agent. The company shall at all times have a registered agent and registered office. The initial registered agent and registered office shall be listed on Schedule A.

8. Assets. The assets of the company shall be registered in the legal name of the company and not in the names of the individual members.

9. Records and Accounting. The company shall keep an accurate accounting of its affairs using any method of accounting allowed by law. All members shall have a right to inspect the records during normal business hours. The members shall have the power to hire such accountants as they deem necessary or desirable.

10. Banking. The members of the company shall be authorized to set up bank accounts as in their sole discretion are deemed necessary and are authorized to execute any banking resolutions provided by the institution in which the accounts are being set up.

11. Taxes. The company shall file such tax returns as required by law. The company shall elect to be taxed as a majority of the members decide is in their best interests. The "tax matters partner," as required by the Internal Revenue Code, shall be listed on Schedule A.

12. Separate Entity. The company is a legal entity separate from its members. No member shall have any separate liability for any debts, obligations, or liability of the company except as provided in this agreement.

13. Indemnity and Exculpation. The limited liability company shall indemnify and hold harmless its members, managers, employees, and agents to the fullest extent allowed by law for acts or omissions done as part of their duties to or for the company. Indemnification shall include all liabilities, expenses, attorney and accountant fees, and other costs reasonably expended. No member shall be liable to the company for acts done in good faith.

14. Meetings. The members shall have no obligation to hold annual or any other meeting, but may hold such meetings if they deem them necessary or desirable.

15. Amendment of this Agreement. This agreement may not be amended except in writing signed by all of the members.

16. Conflict of Interest. No member shall be involved with any business or undertaking which competes with the interests of the company except upon agreement in writing by all of the members.

17. Deadlock. In the event that the members cannot come to an agreement on any matter the members agree to submit the issue to mediation to be paid for by the company. In the event the mediation is unsuccessful, they agree to seek arbitration under the rules of the American Arbitration Association.

18. Dissociation of a Member. A member shall have the right to discontinue membership upon giving thirty days notice. A member shall cease to have the right to membership upon death, court-ordered incapacity, bankruptcy or expulsion. The company shall have the right to buy the interest of any dissociated member at fair market value.

19. Dissolution. The company shall dissolve upon the unanimous consent of all the members or upon any event requiring dissolution under state law. In the event of the death, bankruptcy, permanent incapacity, or withdrawal of a member the remaining members may elect to dissolve or to continue the operation of the company.

20. General Provisions. This agreement is intended to represent the entire agreement between the parties. In the event that any party of this agreement is held to be contrary to law or unenforceable, said party shall be considered amended to comply with the law and such holding shall not affect the enforceability of other terms of this agreement. This agreement shall be binding upon the heirs, successors and assigns of the members.

21. Miscellaneous. _____

_____

_____

_____

_____

_____

IN WITNESS whereof, the members of the limited liability company sign this agreement and adopt it as their operating agreement this _____ day of _____, _____.

_____   _____

_____   _____

_____   _____

SCHEDULE A
TO LIMITED LIABILITY COMPANY
OPERATING OR MANAGEMENT AGREEMENT OF

_____

1. Initial member(s): The initial member(s) are:

2. Capital contribution(s): The capital contribution(s) of the member(s) is/are:

3. Profits and losses: The profits, losses, and other tax matters shall be allocated among the members in the following percentages:

4. Management: The company shall be managed by:

5. Registered Agent: The initial registered agent and registered office of the company are:

6. The tax matters partner is:

This page intentionally left blank.

MINUTES OF A MEETING OF MEMBERS OF

_____

A meeting of the members of the company was held on _____, at
_____.

The following were present, being all the members of the limited liability company:

_____   _____

_____   _____

_____   _____

The meeting was called to order and it was moved, seconded, and unanimously carried that
_____ act as Chairman and that _____
act as Secretary.

After discussion and upon motion duly made, seconded, and carried the following resolution(s) were adopted:

There being no further business to come before the meeting, upon motion duly made, seconded, and unanimously
carried, it was adjourned.

_____
Secretary

Members:

_____

_____

_____

_____

This page intentionally left blank.

CERTIFICATE OF AUTHORITY
FOR

_____

This is to certify that the above Limited Liability Company is managed by its

❏ members

❏ managers

who are listed below and that each of them is authorized and empowered to transact business on behalf of the company.

Name

Address

_____

_____

_____

_____

_____

_____

_____

_____

_____

_____

Date: _____

Name of company:

_____

By: _____

Position: _____

This page intentionally left blank.

BANKING RESOLUTION OF

_____

The undersigned, being a member of the above limited liability company authorized to sign this resolution, hereby certifies that on the _____ day of _____, _____ the members of the limited liability company adopted the following resolution:

RESOLVED   that   the   limited   liability   company   open   bank   accounts   with _____ and that the members of the company are authorized to take such action as is necessary to open such accounts; that the bank's printed form of resolution is hereby adopted and incorporated into these minutes by reference; that any _____ of the following person(s) shall have signature authority over the account:

_____   _____

_____   _____;

and, that said resolution has not been modified or rescinded.

Date: _____

_____
Authorized member

This page intentionally left blank.

RESOLUTION
OF

_____

A LIMITED LIABILITY COMPANY

RESOLVED that the company elects to be taxed as follows:

❑ a single member electing to disregard the separate entity

❑ a multiple member entity electing to be taxed as a partnership

❑ a multiple member entity electing to be taxed as a corporation

for tax purposes under the Internal Revenue Code and that the managers or managing members of the limited liability company are directed to file IRS Form 8832 and to take any further action necessary for the company to qualify for said tax status.

Members' Consent

The undersigned shareholders being all of the members of the above limited liability company hereby consent to the above tax election.

Date:_____

Name of member	Percentage owned	Signature
_____	_____	_____
_____	_____	_____
_____	_____	_____
_____	_____	_____

This page intentionally left blank.

CERTIFICATE OF AMENDMENT
TO
ARTICLES OF ORGANIZATION
OF

_____

A LIMITED LIABILITY COMPANY

First: The date of filing of the original Articles of Organization was: _____

Second: The following amendment(s) to the Articles of Organization was/were duly adopted by the limited liability company:

Date: _____

_____

_____

This page intentionally left blank.

CHANGE OF REGISTERED AGENT AND/OR REGISTERED OFFICE

1.   The name of the limited liability company is:

2.   The street address of the current registered office is:

3.   The new address of the registered office is to be:

4.   The current registered agent is:

5.   The new registered agent is:

6.   The street address of the registered office and the street address of the business address of the registered agent are identical.

7.   Such change was duly authorized by the members of the limited liability company.

_____

Having been named as registered agent and to accept service of process for the above stated limited liability company at the place designated in this certificate, I hereby accept the appointment as registered agent and agree to act in this capacity. I further agree to comply with the provisions of all statutes relating to the proper and complete performance of my duties, and am familiar with and accept the obligations of my position as registered agent.

_____
Registered Agent

Index

About the Author

Mark Warda received his B.A. in Political Science from the University of Illinois in Chicago and his J.D. from the University of Illinois in Champaign. He has studied in Barcelona, Cologne, and at the University of Oxford, England. Living in Florida with his wife and young son, he has written or coauthored over sixty self-help law books, including:

The Complete Book of Personal Legal Forms

*How to Form a Limited Liability Company
   in Florida*

How to Form a Nonprofit Corporation

How to Form Your Own Corporation

How to Form Your Own Corporation in Florida

*How to Form Your Own Corporation
   in Massachusetts*

How to Form Your Own Corporation in Minnesota

How to Form Your Own Corporation in New York

How to Form Your Own Corporation in Ohio

How to Register Your Own Copyright

How to Register Your Own Trademark

How to Start a Business in California

How to Start a Business in Florida

How to Start a Business in Georgia

How to Start a Business in Illinois

*How to Start a Business in Maryland, Virginia
   or the District of Columbia*

How to Start a Business in Massachusetts

How to Start a Business in Michigan

How to Start a Business in New York

How to Start a Business in Pennsylvania

How to Start a Business in Texas

INVALUABLE SMALL BUSINESS MANAGEMENT RESOURCES

Your #1 Source for Real World Legal Information...

SPHINX® PUBLISHING
An Imprint of Sourcebooks, Inc.®

- Written by lawyers
- Simple English explanation of the law
- Forms and instructions included

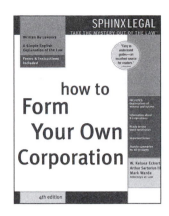

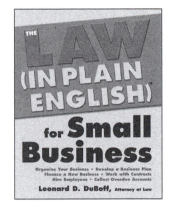

How to Form Your own Corporation, 4E

This book explores the fundamental tasks of starting your own corporation. A valuable resource for anyone who wants to form a corporation, with state-by-state incorporation laws and ready-to-use forms.

216 pages; $26.95;
ISBN 1-57248-345-8

The Complete Book of Personal Legal Forms

Getting the right legal forms can cost you thousands of dollars in attorney's fees—but using the wrong forms can cost you even more. This title provides you with over 110 common forms everyone can use.

400 pages; $24.95;
ISBN 1-57248-499-3

The Law (in Plain English) for Small Business

A concise guide that covers every legal topic concerning a small business owner. From hiring procedures to product liability, this book provides answers in simple, everyday language.

320 pages; $19.95;
ISBN 1-57248-337-6

See the following order form for books written specifically for California, the District of Columbia, Florida, Georgia, Illinois, Maryland, Massachusetts, Michigan, Minnesota, New Jersey, New York, North Carolina, Ohio, Pennsylvania, Texas, and Virginia!

What our customers say about our books:

"It couldn't be more clear for the lay person." —R.D.

"I want you to know I really appreciate your book. It has saved me a lot of time and money." —L.T.

"Your real estate contracts book has saved me nearly $12,000.00 in closing costs over the past year." —A.B.

"...many of the legal questions that I have had over the years were answered clearly and concisely through your plain English interpretation of the law." —C.E.H.

"If there weren't people out there like you I'd be lost. You have the best books of this type out there." —S.B.

"...your forms and directions are easy to follow." —C.V.M.

Sphinx Publishing's Legal Survival Guides
are directly available from Sourcebooks, Inc., or from your local bookstores.

For credit card orders call 1–800–432–7444, write P.O. Box 4410, Naperville, IL 60567-4410,
or fax 630-961-2168
Find more legal information at: **www.SphinxLegal.com**

SPHINX® PUBLISHING'S STATE TITLES

Up-to-Date for Your State

California Titles

How to File for Divorce in CA (5E)	$26.95
How to Settle & Probate an Estate in CA (2E)	$28.95
How to Start a Business in CA (2E)	$21.95
How to Win in Small Claims Court in CA (2E)	$18.95
The Landlord's Legal Guide in CA (2E)	$24.95
Make Your Own CA Will	$18.95
Tenants' Rights in CA	$21.95

Florida Titles

How to File for Divorce in FL (8E)	$28.95
How to Form a Corporation in FL (6E)	$24.95
How to Form a Limited Liability Co. in FL (3E)	$24.95
How to Form a Partnership in FL	$22.95
How to Make a FL Will (7E)	$16.95
How to Probate and Settle an Estate in FL (5E)	$26.95
How to Start a Business in FL (7E)	$21.95
How to Win in Small Claims Court in FL (7E)	$18.95
Land Trusts in Florida (6E)	$29.95
Landlords' Rights and Duties in FL (9E)	$22.95

Georgia Titles

How to File for Divorce in GA (5E)	$21.95
How to Make a GA Will (4E)	$16.95
How to Start a Business in Georgia (3E)	$21.95

Illinois Titles

Child Custody, Visitation and Support in IL	$24.95
How to File for Divorce in IL (3E)	$24.95
How to Make an IL Will (3E)	$16.95
How to Start a Business in IL (4E)	$21.95
The Landlord's Legal Guide in IL	$24.95

Maryland, Virginia and the District of Columbia Titles

How to File for Divorce in MD, VA and DC	$28.95
How to Start a Business in MD, VA or DC	$21.95

Massachusetts Titles

How to Form a Corporation in MA	$24.95
How to Make a MA Will (2E)	$16.95
How to Start a Business in MA (4E)	$21.95
The Landlord's Legal Guide in MA (2E)	$24.95

Michigan Titles

How to File for Divorce in MI (4E)	$24.95
How to Make a MI Will (3E)	$16.95
How to Start a Business in MI (4E)	$24.95

Minnesota Titles
How to File for Divorce in MN	$21.95
How to Form a Corporation in MN	$24.95
How to Make a MN Will (2E)	$16.95

New Jersey Titles
How to File for Divorce in NJ	$24.95
How to Start a Business in NJ	$21.95

New York Titles
Child Custody, Visitation and Support in NY	$26.95
File for Divorce in NY	$26.95
How to Form a Corporation in NY (3E)	$21.95
How to Make a NY Will (3E)	$16.95
How to Start a Business in NY (2E)	$18.95
How to Win in Small Claims Court in NY (2E)	$18.95
Landlords' Legal Guide in NY	$24.95
Tenants' Rights in NY	$21.95

North Carolina and South Carolina Titles
How to File for Divorce in NC (3E)	$22.95
How to Make a NC Will (3E)	$16.95
How to Start a Business in NC or SC	$24.95
Landlords' Rights & Duties in NC	$21.95

Ohio Titles
How to File for Divorce in OH (3E)	$24.95
How to Form a Corporation in OH	$24.95
How to Make an OH Will	$16.95

Pennsylvania Titles
Child Custody, Visitation and Support in PA	$26.95
How to File for Divorce in PA (4E)	$24.95
How to Form a Corporation in PA	$24.95
How to Make a PA Will (2E)	$16.95
How to Start a Business in PA (3E)	$21.95
The Landlord's Legal Guide in PA	$24.95

Texas Titles
Child Custody, Visitation and Support in TX	$22.95
How to File for Divorce in TX (4E)	$24.95
How to Form a Corporation in TX (3E)	$24.95
How to Make a TX Will (3E)	$16.95
How to Probate and Settle an Estate in TX (4E)	$26.95
How to Start a Business in TX (4E)	$21.95
How to Win in Small Claims Court in TX (2E)	$16.95
The Landlord's Legal Guide in TX	$24.95

Sphinx® Publishing's National Titles
Valid in All 50 States

LEGAL SURVIVAL IN BUSINESS

The Complete Book of Corporate Forms	$24.95
The Complete Hiring and Firing Handbookk	$19.95
The Complete Limited Liability Kit	$21.95
The Complete Partnership Book	$24.95
The Complete Patent Book	$26.95
Employees' Rights	$18.95
Employer's Rights	$24.95
The Entrepreneur's Internet Handbook	$21.95
The Entrepreneur's Legal Guide	$26.95
Financing Your Small Business	$17.95
Fired, Laid-Off or Forced Out	$14.95
How to Buy a Franchise	$19.95
How to Form a Limited Liability Company (2E)	$24.95
How to Form a Nonprofit Corporation (3E)	$24.95
How to Form Your Own Corporation (4E)	$26.95
How to Register Your Own Copyright (5E)	$24.95
How to Register Your Own Trademark (3E)	$21.95
Incorporate in Delaware from Any State	$26.95
Incorporate in Nevada from Any State	$24.95
The Law (In Plain English)® for Small Business	$19.95
The Law (In Plain English)® for Writers	$16.95
Minding Her Own Business, 4E	$14.95
Most Valuable Business Legal Forms You'll Ever Need (3E)	$21.95
Profit from Intellectual Property	$28.95
Protect Your Patent	$24.95
The Small Business Owner's Guide to Bankruptcy	$21.95
Tax Power for the Self-Eemployed	$17.95
Tax Smarts for Small Business	$21.95

LEGAL SURVIVAL IN COURT

Attorney Responsibilities & Client Rights	$19.95
Crime Victim's Guide to Justice (2E)	$21.95
Legal Research Made Easy (3E)	$21.95
Winning Your Personal Injury Claim (3E)	$24.95

LEGAL SURVIVAL IN REAL ESTATE

The Complete Kit to Selling Your Own Home	$18.95
Essential Guide to Real Estate Contracts (2E)	$18.95
Essential Guide to Real Estate Leases	$18.95
Homeowner's Rights	$19.95
How to Buy a Condominium or Townhome (2E)	$19.95
How to Buy Your First Home (2E)	$14.95
The Mortgage Answer Book	$14.95
The Weekend Landlord	$16.95
Working with Your Homeowners Association	$19.95

LEGAL SURVIVAL IN SPANISH

Cómo Comprar su Primera Casa	$8.95
Cómo Hacer su Propio Testamento	$16.95
Cómo Negociar su Crédito	$8.95
Cómo Organizar un Presupuesto	$8.95
Cómo Solicitar su Propio Divorcio	$24.95
Guía de Inmigración a Estados Unidos (4E)	$24.95
Guía de Justicia para Víctimas del Crimen	$21.95
Guía Esencial para los Contratos de Arrendamiento de Bienes Raices	$22.95

Inmigración y Ciudadanía en los EE. UU. Preguntas y Respuestas	$16.95
Inmigración a los EE. UU. Paso a Paso (2E)	$24.95
Manual de Beneficios para el Seguro Social	$18.95
El Seguro Social Preguntas y Respuestas	$16.95

LEGAL SURVIVAL IN PERSONAL AFFAIRS

101 Complaint Letters That Get Results	$18.95
The 529 College Savings Plan (2E)	$18.95
The 529 College Savings Plan Made Simple	$7.95
The Alternative Minimum Tax	$14.95
The Antique and Art Collector's Legal Guide	$24.95
Child Support	$18.95
The Complete Adoption and Fertility Legal Guide	$24.95
The Complete Book of Insurance	$18.95
The Complete Book of Personal Legal Forms	$24.95
The Complete Legal Guide to Senior Care	$21.95
Credit Smart	$18.95
Fathers' Rights	$19.95
Family Limited Partnership	$26.95
The Frequent Traveler's Guide	$14.95
Gay & Lesbian Rights	$26.95
Grandparents' Rights (3E)	$24.95
How to File Your Own Bankruptcy (6E)	$21.95
How to File Your Own Divorce (5E)	$26.95
How to Make Your Own Simple Will (3E)	$18.95
How to Parent with Your Ex	$12.95
How to Write Your Own Living Will (4E)	$18.95
How to Write Your Own Premarital Agreement (3E)	$24.95
Law 101	$16.95
Law School 101	$16.95
The Living Trust Kit	$21.95
Living Trusts and Other Ways to Avoid Probate (3E)	$24.95
Mastering the MBE	$16.95
Nursing Homes and Assisted Living Facilities	$19.95
The Power of Attorney Handbook (5E)	$22.95
Repair Your Own Credit and Deal with Debt (2E)	$18.95
Quick Cash	$14.95
Sexual Harassment:Your Guide to Legal Action	$18.95
Seniors' Rights	$19.95
Sisters-in-Law	$16.95
The Social Security Benefits Handbook (4E)	$18.95
Social Security Q&A	$12.95
Starting Our or Starting Over	$14.95
Teen Rights	$22.95
Unmarried Parents' Rights (2E)	$19.95
U.S. Immigration and Citizenship Q&A	$18.95
U.S. Immigration Step by Step (2E)	$24.95
U.S.A. Immigration Guide (5E)	$26.95
What to Do—Before "I DO"	$14.95
The Wills, Estate Planning and Trusts Legal Kit	$26.95
Win Your Unemployment Compensation Claim (2E)	$21.95
Your Right to Child Custody, Visitation and Support (3E)	$24.95

SPHINX® PUBLISHING ORDER FORM

BILL TO:		SHIP TO:	
Phone #	**Terms**	**F.O.B.** Chicago, IL	**Ship Date**

Charge my: ☐ VISA ☐ MasterCard ☐ American Express

☐ **Money Order or Personal Check**

Credit Card Number

Expiration Date

Qty	ISBN	Title	Retail	Ext.	Qty	ISBN	Title	Retail	Ext.
		SPHINX PUBLISHING NATIONAL TITLES				1-57248-379-2	How to Register Your Own Copyright (5E)	$24.95	
____	1-57248-363-6	101 Complaint Letters That Get Results	$18.95		____	1-57248-104-8	How to Register Your Own Trademark (3E)	$21.95	
____	1-57248-361-X	The 529 College Savings Plan (2E)	$18.95		____	1-57248-394-6	How to Write Your Own Living Will (4E)	$18.95	
____	1-57248-483-7	The 529 College Savings Plan Made Simple	$7.95		____	1-57248-156-0	How to Write Your Own Premarital Agreement (3E)	$24.95	
____	1-57248-460-8	The Alternative Minimum Tax	$14.95		____	1-57248-230-3	Incorporate in Delaware from Any State	$26.95	
____	1-57248-349-0	The Antique and Art Collector's Legal Guide	$24.95		____	1-57248-158-7	Incorporate in Nevada from Any State	$24.95	
____	1-57248-347-4	Attorney Responsibilities & Client Rights	$19.95		____	1-57248-474-8	Inmigración a los EE.UU. Paso a Paso (2E)	$24.95	
____	1-57248-382-2	Child Support	$18.95		____	1-57248-400-4	Inmigración y Ciudadanía en los EE.UU. Preguntas y Respuestas	$16.95	
____	1-57248-487-X	Cómo Comprar su Primera Casa	$8.95						
____	1-57248-148-X	Cómo Hacer su Propio Testamento	$16.95		____	1-57248-453-5	Law 101	$16.95	
____	1-57248-462-4	Cómo Negociar su Crédito	$8.95		____	1-57248-374-1	Law School 101	$16.95	
____	1-57248-463-2	Cómo Organizar un Presupuesto	$8.95		____	1-57248-377-6	The Law (In Plain English)® for Small Business	$19.95	
____	1-57248-147-1	Cómo Solicitar su Propio Divorcio	$24.95		____	1-57248-476-4	The Law (In Plain English)® for Writers	$16.95	
____	1-57248-373-3	The Complete Adoption and Fertility Legal Guide	$24.95		____	1-57248-223-0	Legal Research Made Easy (3E)	$21.95	
____	1-57248-166-8	The Complete Book of Corporate Forms	$24.95		____	1-57248-449-7	The Living Trust Kit	$21.95	
____	1-57248-383-0	The Complete Book of Insurance	$18.95		____	1-57248-165-X	Living Trusts and Other Ways to Avoid Probate (3E)	$24.95	
____	1-57248499-3	The Complete Book of Personal Legal Forms	$24.95						
____	1-57248-458-6	The Complete Hiring and Firing Handbook	$18.95		____	1-57248-186-2	Manual de Beneficios para el Seguro Social	$18.95	
____	1-57248-353-9	The Complete Kit to Selling Your Own Home	$18.95		____	1-57248-220-6	Mastering the MBE	$16.95	
____	1-57248-229-X	The Complete Legal Guide to Senior Care	$21.95		____	1-57248-455-1	Minding Her Own Business, 4E	$14.95	
____	1-57248-498-5	The Complete Limited Liability Company Kit	$21.95		____	1-57248-480-2	The Mortgage Answer Book	$14.95	
____	1-57248-391-1	The Complete Partnership Book	$24.95		____	1-57248-167-6	Most Val. Business Legal Forms You'll Ever Need (3E)	$21.95	
____	1-57248-201-X	The Complete Patent Book	$26.95						
____	1-57248-480-2	The Mortgage Answer Book	$14.95		____	1-57248-388-1	The Power of Attorney Handbook (5E)	$22.95	
____	1-57248-369-5	Credit Smart	$18.95		____	1-57248-332-6	Profit from Intellectual Property	$28.95	
____	1-57248-163-3	Crime Victim's Guide to Justice (2E)	$21.95		____	1-57248-329-6	Protect Your Patent	$24.95	
____	1-57248-367-9	Employees' Rights	$18.95		____	1-57248-376-8	Nursing Homes and Assisted Living Facilities	$19.95	
____	1-57248-365-2	Employer's Rights	$24.95		____	1-57248-385-7	Quick Cash	$14.95	
____	1-57248-251-6	The Entrepreneur's Internet Handbook	$21.95		____	1-57248-344-X	Repair Your Own Credit and Deal with Debt (2E)	$18.95	
____	1-57248-235-4	The Entrepreneur's Legal Guide	$26.95		____	1-57248-350-4	El Seguro Social Preguntas y Respuestas	$16.95	
____	1-57248-346-6	Essential Guide to Real Estate Contracts (2E)	$18.95		____	1-57248386-5	Seniors' Rights	$19.95	
____	1-57248-160-9	Essential Guide to Real Estate Leases	$18.95		____	1-57248-217-6	Sexual Harassment: Your Guide to Legal Action	$18.95	
____	1-57248-254-0	Family Limited Partnership	$26.95		____	1-57248-378-4	Sisters-in-Law	$16.95	
____	1-57248-375-X	Fathers' Rights	$19.95		____	1-57248-219-2	The Small Business Owner's Guide to Bankruptcy	$21.95	
____	1-57248-450-0	Financing Your Small Business	$17.95		____	1-57248-395-4	The Social Security Benefits Handbook (4E)	$18.95	
____	1-57248-459-4	Fired, Laid Off or Forced Out	$14.95		____	1-57248-216-8	Social Security Q&A	$12.95	
____	1-57248-502-7	The Frequent Traveler's Guide	$14.95		____	1-57248-328-8	Starting Out or Starting Over	$14.95	
____	1-57248-331-8	Gay & Lesbian Rights	$26.95		____	1-57248-221-4	Teen Rights	$22.95	
____	1-57248-139-0	Grandparents' Rights (3E)	$24.95		____	1-57248-457-8	Tax Power for the Self-Employed	$17.95	
____	1-57248-475-6	Guía de Inmigración a Estados Unidos (4E)	$24.95		____	1-57248-366-0	Tax Smarts for Small Business	$21.95	
____	1-57248-187-0	Guía de Justicia para Víctimas del Crimen	$21.95		____	1-57248-236-2	Unmarried Parents' Rights (2E)	$19.95	
____	1-57248-253-2	Guía Esencial para los Contratos de Arrendamiento de Bienes Raices	$22.95		____	1-57248-362-8	U.S. Immigration and Citizenship Q&A	$18.95	
					____	1-57248-387-3	U.S. Immigration Step by Step (2E)	$24.95	
____	1-57248-334-2	Homeowner's Rights	$19.95		____	1-57248-392-X	U.S.A. Immigration Guide (5E)	$26.95	
____	1-57248-164-1	How to Buy a Condominium or Townhome (2E)	$19.95		____	1-57248-177-2	The Weekend Landlord	$16.95	
____	1-57248-197-7	How to Buy Your First Home (2E)	$14.95		____	1-57248-451-9	What to Do — Before "I DO"	$14.95	
____	1-57248-384-9	How to Buy a Franchise	$19.95		____	1-57248-225-7	Win Your Unemployment Compensation Claim (2E)	$21.95	
____	1-57248-472-1	How to File Your Own Bankruptcy (6E)	$21.95						
____	1-57248-343-1	How to File Your Own Divorce (5E)	$26.95		____	1-57248-330-X	The Wills, Estate Planning and Trusts Legal Kit	$26.95	
____	1-57248-222-2	How to Form a Limited Liability Company (2E)	$24.95		____	1-57248-473-X	Winning Your Personal Injury Claim (3E)	$24.95	
____	1-57248-390-3	How to Form a Nonprofit Corporation (3E)	$24.95		____	1-57248-333-4	Working with Your Homeowners Association	$19.95	
____	1-57248-345-8	How to Form Your Own Corporation (4E)	$26.95		____	1-57248-380-6	Your Right to Child Custody, Visitation and Support (3E)	$24.95	
____	1-57248-232-X	How to Make Your Own Simple Will (3E)	$18.95						
____	1-57248-479-9	How to Parent with Your Ex	$12.95				**Total for this page**		____

To order, call Sourcebooks at 1-800-432-7444 or FAX (630) 961-2168 (Bookstores, libraries, wholesalers—please call for discount)

Prices are subject to change without notice.

Find more legal information at: **www.SphinxLegal.com**

SPHINX® PUBLISHING ORDER FORM

Qty	ISBN	Title	Retail	Ext.
		CALIFORNIA TITLES		
____	1-57248-489-6	How to File for Divorce in CA (5E)	$26.95	____
____	1-57248-464-0	How to Settle and Probate an Estate in CA	$28.95	____
____	1-57248-336-9	How to Start a Business in CA (2E)	$21.95	____
____	1-57248-194-3	How to Win in Small Claims Court in CA (2E)	$18.95	____
____	1-57248-246-X	Make Your Own CA Will	$18.95	____
____	1-57248-397-0	The Landlord's Legal Guide in CA (2E)	$24.95	____
____	1-57248-241-9	Tenants' Rights in CA	$21.95	____
		FLORIDA TITLES		
____	1-57248-396-2	How to File for Divorce in FL (8E)	$28.95	____
____	1-57248-356-3	How to Form a Corporation in FL (6E)	$24.95	____
____	1-57248-490-X	How to Form a Limited Liability Co. in FL (3E)	$24.95	____
____	1-57071-401-0	How to Form a Partnership in FL	$22.95	____
____	1-57248-456-X	How to Make a FL Will (7E)	$16.95	____
____	1-57248-354-7	How to Probate and Settle an Estate in FL (5E)	$26.95	____
____	1-57248-339-3	How to Start a Business in FL (7E)	$21.95	____
____	1-57248-204-4	How to Win in Small Claims Court in FL (7E)	$18.95	____
____	1-57248-381-4	Land Trusts in Florida (7E)	$29.95	____
____	1-57248-338-5	Landlords' Rights and Duties in FL (9E)	$22.95	____
		GEORGIA TITLES		
____	1-57248-340-7	How to File for Divorce in GA (5E)	$21.95	____
____	1-57248-180-3	How to Make a GA Will (4E)	$16.95	____
____	1-57248-341-5	How to Start a Business in Georgia (3E)	$21.95	____
		ILLINOIS TITLES		
____	1-57248-244-3	Child Custody, Visitation, and Support in IL	$24.95	____
____	1-57248-206-0	How to File for Divorce in IL (3E)	$24.95	____
____	1-57248-170-6	How to Make an IL Will (3E)	$16.95	____
____	1-57248-265-9	How to Start a Business in IL (4E)	$21.95	____
____	1-57248-252-4	The Landlord's Legal Guide in IL	$24.95	____
		MARYLAND, VIRGINIA AND THE DISTRICT OF COLUMBIA		
____	1-57248-240-0	How to File for Divorce in MD, VA and DC	$28.95	____
____	1-57248-359-8	How to Start a Business in MD, VA or DC	$21.95	____
		MASSACHUSETTS TITLES		
____	1-57248-115-3	How to Form a Corporation in MA	$24.95	____
____	1-57248-108-0	How to Make a MA Will (2E)	$16.95	____
____	1-57248-466-7	How to Start a Business in MA (4E)	$21.95	____
____	1-57248-398-9	The Landlord's Legal Guide in MA (2E)	$24.95	____
		MICHIGAN TITLES		
____	1-57248-467-5	How to File for Divorce in MI (4E)	$24.95	____
____	1-57248-182-X	How to Make a MI Will (3E)	$16.95	____
____	1-57248-183-8	How to Start a Business in MI (3E)	$18.95	____
		MINNESOTA TITLES		
____	1-57248-142-0	How to File for Divorce in MN	$21.95	____
____	1-57248-179-X	How to Form a Corporation in MN	$24.95	____
____	1-57248-178-1	How to Make a MN Will (2E)	$16.95	____
		NEW JERSEY TITLES		
____	1-57248-239-7	How to File for Divorce in NJ	$24.95	____
____	1-57248-448-9	How to Start a Business in NJ	$21.95	____
		NEW YORK TITLES		
____	1-57248-193-5	Child Custody, Visitation and Support in NY	$26.95	____
____	1-57248-351-2	File for Divorce in NY	$26.95	____
____	1-57248-249-4	How to Form a Corporation in NY (2E)	$24.95	____
____	1-57248-401-2	How to Make a NY Will (3E)	$16.95	____
____	1-57248-469-1	How to Start a Business in NY (3E)	$21.95	____
____	1-57248-198-6	How to Win in Small Claims Court in NY (2E)	$18.95	____
____	1-57248-197-8	Landlords' Legal Guide in NY	$24.95	____
____	1-57248-122-6	Tenants' Rights in NY	$21.95	____

Qty	ISBN	Title	Retail	Ext.
		NORTH CAROLINA TITLES		
____	1-57248-185-4	How to File for Divorce in NC (3E)	$22.95	____
____	1-57248-129-3	How to Make a NC Will (3E)	$16.95	____
____	1-57248-184-6	How to Start a Business in NC (3E)	$18.95	____
____	1-57248-091-2	Landlords' Rights & Duties in NC	$21.95	____
		NORTH CAROLINA AND SOUTH CAROLINA TITLES		
____	1-57248-371-7	How to Start a Business in NC or SC	$24.95	____
		OHIO TITLES		
____	1-57248-503-5	How to File for Divorce in OH (3E)	$24.95	____
____	1-57248-174-9	How to Form a Corporation in OH	$24.95	____
____	1-57248-173-0	How to Make an OH Will	$16.95	____
		PENNSYLVANIA TITLES		
____	1-57248-242-7	Child Custody, Visitation and Support in PA	$26.95	____
____	1-57248-495-0	How to File for Divorce in PA (4E)	$24.95	____
____	1-57248-358-X	How to Form a Cooporation in PA	$24.95	____
____	1-57248-094-7	How to Make a PA Will (2E)	$16.95	____
____	1-57248-357-1	How to Start a Business in PA (3E)	$21.95	____
____	1-57248-245-1	The Landlord's Legal Guide in PA	$24.95	____
		TEXAS TITLES		
____	1-57248-171-4	Child Custody, Visitation, and Support in TX	$22.95	____
____	1-57248-399-7	How to File for Divorce in TX (4E)	$24.95	____
____	1-57248-470-5	How to Form a Corporation in TX (3E)	$24.95	____
____	1-57248-255-9	How to Make a TX Will (3E)	$16.95	____
____	1-57248-496-9	How to Probate and Settle an Estate in TX (4E)	$26.95	____
____	1-57248-471-3	How to Start a Business in TX (4E)	$21.95	____
____	1-57248-111-0	How to Win in Small Claims Court in TX (2E)	$16.95	____
____	1-57248-355-5	The Landlord's Legal Guide in TX	$24.95	____

SubTotal This page ____

SubTotal previous page ____

Shipping— $5.00 for 1st book, $1.00 each additional ____

Illinois residents add 6.75% sales tax ____

Connecticut residents add 6.00% sales tax ____

Total ____

To order, call Sourcebooks at 1-800-432-7444 or FAX (630) 961-2168 (Bookstores, libraries, wholesalers—please call for discount)

Prices are subject to change without notice.

Find more legal information at: **www.SphinxLegal.com**

TERMS AND DISCOUNT POLICIES

To order, call (800) 43-BRIGHT, (630) 961-3900 or FAX to (630) 961-2168
Email: info@sourcebooks.com

Returnable Retail and Retail Distribution Center Discount

Sourcebooks, Sourcebooks Landmark, Sourcebooks MediaFusion, Sourcebooks Casablanca, Sourcebooks Hysteria, Sphinx Publishing, Good Year Books, Longman Publishers and Prufrock Press orders automatically combine for best discount.

Assorted Quantity	Drop-Ship Discount	RDC Discount
1-4	20%	20%
5-9	40%	40%
10+	46%	48%

50% discount on all PREPACKS

A retail distribution center (RDC) is a centralized distribution facility or facilities, maintained by a retailer, for the purpose of warehousing and shipping books to three or more locations. Orders picked and packed for individual stores and shipped to a distribution center will not be eligible for the RDC discount. All RDC orders must be in carton quantities.

STOP and Prepaid orders

Assorted Quantity	Discount
1-4	30% (shipping: $5.00 for first book, $1.00 each additional)
5+	Drop ship discount and FREE FREIGHT

Library Standard Discount 15%
Standing Orders 30%

Course Adoption

Free examination copy requests must be sent on university letterhead to: Sourcebooks, Inc., 1935 Brookdale Rd., Ste. 139, Naperville, IL 60563 or faxed to (630) 961-2168.

ORDERS

Please send all orders to: Sourcebooks, Inc., 1935 Brookdale Rd., Ste. 139, Naperville, IL 60563. Toll-free phone (800) 432-7444. Fax (630) 961-2168. Terms are net 30. Payments in excess of $10,000 paid by credit card are subject to a 3% processing fee at time of payment. All orders ship FOB origin from Aurora, Illinois. Prices and policies are subject to change without notice.

RETURNS

Please send all returns, freight prepaid, to: Sourcebooks, Inc., 940 Enterprise St., Aurora, IL 60504. Credit will not be given for OP books, damaged books or books not published by Sourcebooks, Inc. All returns will be credited at 50% unless original invoice information is provided. Claims for incorrect or damaged shipments must be made within 30 days from the invoice date.

ISBN PREFIXES: 1-4022, 1-57071, 1-57248, 1-883518, 1-887166, 0-913825, 0-942061, 0-9629162

SOURCEBOOKS, INC., IS REPRESENTED TO THE TRADE BY:

Canada:
Canadian Manda Group
(Carey Low, Sales Manager)
(416) 516-0911
Fax: (416) 516-0917
clow@mandagroup.com

Mid-Atlantic:
Sirak & Sirak Associates
(Jim Sirak, Lisa Sirak, Frank Porter, Marel Dryl)
(973) 299-0085
Fax:(973) 263-2363
siraksirak@aol.com

Midwest:
Heinecken & Associates
(Ted Heinecken, Barbara Aronson, Charles Boswell, Wes Caliger, Beth Chang, Robert McLaughlin)
(800) 449-0138
Fax: (800) 947-5694
thein@sprintmail.com

New England:
Nanci McCrackin
(603) 924-8766
Fax: (603) 924-0096
mcbooks@aol.com

Northwest:
Redsides Publishing Services
(George Carroll)
(425) 922-1045
Fax: (425) 671-0362
george@redsides.com

South:
George Scheer Associates
(Wayne Donnell, Tom Murphy, Elaine Rathgeber, Nathan Carter)
(800) 265-8504 • (336) 855-1374
Fax: (336) 854-6908
wrdonnell@aol.com

West:
Thomas McFadden & Associates
(Thomas McFadden, Bob Ditter, Susan Zevnik, Susan Hughes)
(303) 771-2898
Fax: (303) 771-4909
tmcfadden@msn.com

FOREIGN DISTRIBUTION

Contact:
Anne Landa, Rights & Exports Sales Manager
Tel: (630) 961-3900 ext. 229
email: anne.landa@sourcebooks.com

FOREIGN AGENTS — Sourcebooks, Inc., is represented by:

Brazil (Portuguese):
Karin Schindler
Tel: 55 11 504 19177
Fax: 55 11 504 19077
kschind@terra.com.br

France & Quebec (French):
Eliane Benisti
Agence Eliane Benisti
Tel: 33 14 22 285 33
Fax: 33 14 54 41 817
benisti@compuserve.com

Germany (German):
Joachin Jessen
Thomas Schluek Agency
Tel: 49 513 14 97562
Fax: 49 513 14 97589
j.jessen@schlueckagent.com

Israel (Hebrew):
Harris/Elon Agency
Tel: 972 2 563 3237
Fax: 972 2 561 8711
litagent@netvision.net.il

Italy (Italian):
Piergiorgio Nicolazzini
Piergiorgio Nicolazzini Agency
Tel: 39 02 487 13365
Fax: 39 02 487 13365
piergiorgio.nicolazzini@tin.it

Japan (Japanese):
Manami Tamaoki
Tuttle-Mori Agency
Tel: 81 3 3230 4081
Fax: 81 3 3234 5249
manami@tuttlemori.com

Korea (Korean):
Inter-Ko
Tel: 82 26 074 724
Fax: 82 26 074 726
sinterko@chollian.net

Russia, Poland, Czech, Slovak, Greece, Bulgaria, Hungary, Slovenia, Croatia, Romania, Baltic, Lithuania, Estonia, Latvia
Prava I Prevodi
Belgrade, Yugoslavia
Tel: 381 11 460 290, 462 662
Fax: 381 11 472 146, 344 2887
rights@pip.co.yu

Spain and Portugal (Spanish, Catalan, Portuguese):
Julio F Yañez
Agencia Literaria
Tel: 349 3200 71 07
Fax: 349 3209 48 65
yanezag@retemail.es

Note: When you see [icon] it means that the book will fit nicely on our new black easel displays. The number reflects how many of that title will fit in the display. Use Item# EAS002 on the order form or denote the quantity of Item# EAS002 easels on your order.

How to Use the CD-ROM

Thank you for purchasing *The Complete Limited Liability Kit (+ CD-ROM)*. An LLC provides any size business with a wealth of advantages in terms of liability protection and asset management. This book gives you exactly what you need to use those advantages to your greatest benefit. To make this material even more useful, we have included every document in the book on the CD-ROM that is attached to the inside back cover of the book.

You can use these forms just as you would the forms in the book. Print them out, fill them in, and use them however you need. You can also fill in the forms directly on your computer. Just identify the form you need, open it, click on the space where the information should go, and input your information. Customize each form for your particular needs. Use them over and over again.

The CD-ROM is compatible with both PC and Mac operating systems. (While it should work with either operating system, we cannot guarantee that it will work with your particular system and we cannot provide technical assistance.) To use the forms on your computer, you will need to use Adobe® Reader®. The CD-ROM does not contain this program. You can download this program from Adobe's website at **www.adobe.com**. Click on the "Get Adobe® Reader®" icon to begin the download process and follow the instructions.

Once you have Adobe® Reader® installed, insert the CD-ROM into your computer. Double click on the icon representing the disc on your desktop or go through your hard drive to identify the drive that contains the disc and click on it.

Once opened, you will see the files contained on the CD-ROM listed as "Form #: [Form Title]." Open the file you need through Adobe® Reader®. You may print the form to fill it out manually at this point, or your can use the "Hand Tool" and click on the appropriate line to fill it in using your computer.

Any time you see bracketed information [ ] on the form, you can click on it and delete the bracketed information from your final form. This information is only a reference guide to assist you in filling in the forms and should be removed from your final version. Once all your information is filled in, you can print your filled-in form.

NOTE: *Adobe® Reader® does not allow you to save the PDF with the boxes filled in.*

. . . .

Purchasers of this book are granted a license to use the forms contained in it for their own personal use. By purchasing this book, you have also purchased a limited license to use all forms on the accompanying CD-ROM. The license limits you to personal use only and all other copyright laws must be adhered. No claim of copyright is made in any government form reproduced in the book or on the CD-ROM. You are free to modify the forms and tailor them to your specific situation.

The author and publisher have attempted to provide the most current and up-to-date information available. However, the courts, Congress, and your state's legislatures review, modify, and change laws on an ongoing basis, as well as create new laws from time to time. By the very nature of the information and due to the continual changes in our legal system, to be sure that you have the current and best information for your situation, you should consult a local attorney or research the current laws yourself.

. . . .

This publication is designed to provide accurate and authoritative information in regard to the subject matter covered. It is sold with the understanding that the publisher is not engaged in rendering legal, accounting, or other professional service. If legal advice or other expert assistance is required, the services of a competent professional person should be sought.

    —From a Declaration of Principles Jointly Adopted by a Committee of the American Bar Association and a Committee of Publishers and Associations

This product is not a substitute for legal advice.

    —Disclaimer required by Texas statutes